Dinner's
on the Table

Many thanks to Wendy Inder for her kitchen skills and to the friends and friends of friends who willingly gave their time to star in *Dinner's on the Table*.

Copyright © in recipes: Jan Bilton, 2008
Copyright © in photography: Jim Tannock, 2008
Copyright © David Bateman Ltd, 2008

First published in 2008 by David Bateman Ltd
30 Tarndale Grove, Albany, Auckland, New Zealand

Conceived and packaged for David Bateman Ltd in 2008 by Renaissance Publishing
PO Box 36 206, Northcote, Auckland

Design: Gina Hochstein
Printed through Bookbuilders, China

Dinner's
on the Table
food for families to eat together

JAN BILTON

David Bateman

CONTENTS

INTRODUCTION

It's true. Home is where the heart is. And family meals are at the heart of a happy home.

WHEN I WAS YOUNGER, dinners were a very enjoyable family get-together. We discussed the day's events and shared our problems and we all felt much better for it. Now it seems that family meals are, in more and more homes, the exception rather than the rule. It is understandable – long working hours for parents, after-work and after-school activities, the distractions of television and computers – but nevertheless regrettable. Dinner is often the only time in the day when family ties can be strengthened; when a sense of 'togetherness' can be experienced.

It is also worth noting that research indicates that meals eaten at the table with the family are healthier, providing better nutritional intake – more vitamins and minerals and less fat. And children who eat with the family tend to consume more fruits and vegetables and fewer fattening snack foods between meals.

- Go shopping together. Let children help choose the vegetables, fruit, meat and/or fish and put it in the supermarket trolley. Discuss the foods so your children are aware that not all food comes out of a freezer or a packet. With a little knowledge they are more likely to attempt to try and to enjoy a new vegetable or other foods.

- Once you are home, ask children to help store the food. They will soon realise which foods are in season and how they should be stored.

- Encourage children to help prepare the vegetables or something simple. Asking them to help may make the prep a little longer, but more often than not they will take pride in their creativity and this encourages other family members to come to the table to try the mutually prepared masterpiece.

- Trying to encourage children of all ages to join in meals at the table can sometimes be a challenge. One tip is to place the food in casseroles or on a platter and let them help themselves. This works especially well with make-your-own tacos or burgers. Children will sometimes eat more than if the food is piled on their dinner plate.

- Keep meals simple, nutritious and interesting. And remember, your children will often be influenced by your own enjoyment of a dish.

Family meals should be fun – an exchange of ideas, conversation and feelings. So turn off that television, computer or video game and come to the table.

Bon appetit

FRYPAN
FLAIR

Rosemary Lamburgers in Bagels

PREPARATION: 15 minutes • COOKING TIME: 10 minutes • SERVES 4

500g lean minced lamb
1¹/2 tablespoons finely chopped
   rosemary
1 tablespoon lemon juice
1 small egg, lightly beaten
freshly ground black pepper to taste

4 bagels, halved
4 tablespoons cream cheese
salad ingredients, eg, lettuce, sliced
   yellow or red pepper (capsicum),
   tomatoes, onion

Combine all the ingredients for the lamburgers and mix well. Form into 4 patties, each about the diameter of a bagel. Refrigerate until ready to cook.

Heat an electric frypan on medium heat. Toast the bagels on the cut side. Place to one side.

Pan-fry the burgers for about 4 minutes on each side or until cooked. Spread the toasted halves of the bagels with cream cheese. Place the salad ingredients on the base of each bagel and top with the burgers. Add more salad and cover with the tops of the bagels.

Can be garnished with a little yoghurt or pesto if preferred.

HINTS
- Frypan/one-pot meals can be complemented with crusty bread or rolls, couscous and salads.
- The cost of cooking a roast and vegetables in an electric frypan is about half the price of cooking the same in a conventional oven.
- An electric pan is usually referred to as a 'frypan'. A conventional pan is called a 'frying' pan.
- Meals prepared in an electric frypan can also be cooked in a frying pan on the hob or element on very low heat.

Funky Roast Chicken

A pre-stuffed chicken could be used in this recipe.

PREPARATION: 15 minutes • COOKING TIME: 1¹/2 hours • SERVES 4-5

1.5kg chicken
salt and pepper to taste

Stuffing
1 large onion, diced
1 tablespoon rice bran oil
1 tablespoon each: chopped rosemary,
    oregano, thyme
^{1}/2 teaspoon sugar
2 thick slices white bread, cubed
1 egg, beaten

2 tablespoons rice bran oil, extra
smoked paprika or paprika to taste
10-12 basil leaves to garnish

HINT
*Rice bran oil has a higher smoke point
than many other oils, making it ideal for
frying.*

Wipe the chicken inside and out with paper towels.
Sprinkle with salt and pepper.

To make the stuffing, sauté the onion in the oil in an
electric frypan until soft. Combine with the herbs, sugar,
bread cubes and egg. Fill the cavity of the chicken with
the stuffing. Tie the bird's legs together neatly with
string to secure the stuffing.

Heat the extra oil in the frypan. Add the chicken and
lightly brown all over on medium heat. Cover and cook
for about 1^1/2 hours on medium-low heat, turning
occasionally during cooking.

Peeled potatoes, kumara or pumpkin could be added
about 45 minutes before the end of cooking.

Garnish with paprika and basil leaves. Great served with
a green salad with cherry tomatoes.

DESSERT SUGGESTION

Orange Parfait
^{3}/4 cup prepared custard
^{1}/2 cup yoghurt
2 oranges, peeled and segmented
4 gingernuts, crushed

Combine the custard and yoghurt. Layer with the oranges in
4-5 glasses. Sprinkle with the gingernut crumbs.

Lamb Tacos with Chilli

PREPARATION: 20 minutes • COOKING TIME: 30 minutes • SERVES 4

600g minced lamb
2 medium onions, chopped
1 tablespoon canola or other
    vegetable oil
1-2 teaspoons chilli paste or to taste
1 teaspoon each: dried marjoram,
    smoked paprika
1 tablespoon Worcestershire sauce
$^1/_2$ cup Mexican-type salsa
8 taco shells

Toppings
2 cups shredded lettuce
1 cup grated tasty cheddar cheese
1 large onion, diced
4 tomatoes, chopped
1 small avocado, peeled stoned and diced
$^3/_4$ cup sour cream
1 cup Mexican-type salsa

HINTS
- Mexican-type salsa is readily available in jars from the supermarket.
- Taco shells can be heated briefly in the microwave or conventional oven before filling.
- Add a bit of fun to the meal. Ask everyone to wear a Mexican sombrero (hat) or drape a colourful cotton scarf over their shoulders.

Brown the meat and onions in the oil in an electric frypan. Add the seasonings and the salsa. Cover and simmer gently for 30 minutes. Add a little water if the mixture dries out too much.

Place the chilli mixture in a hot serving bowl in the centre of the table.

To prepare the tacos, let each person spoon the desired amount of filling into their shell and garnish with a little of each of the toppings. Enjoy immediately.

Tex-Mex Pasta

PREPARATION: 10 minutes • COOKING TIME: 30 minutes • SERVES 4

250g bow tie or other small pasta
*   shapes*
spray oil
2 chorizo sausages, thinly sliced
1 each: large onion, green pepper
*   (capsicum), courgette, diced*
400g can tomatoes in juice
$^3/_4$ cup chicken or vegetable stock
2 cups frozen corn
3-4 tablespoons sliced jalapeno chillies,
*   (optional)*
$^1/_2$ cup each: chopped coriander leaves
*   and stalks, grated mild cheddar*
*   cheese*

HINTS

*   *Jalapenos (pronounced 'hell a pen yo')*
    are mild green chillies available in jars.
*   *Spray oil is ideal when you want to*
    reduce fat because you only need a
    very small amount.

Three-quarters fill an electric frypan with water and bring to the boil. Cook the pasta until just tender. (Alternatively, cook conventionally in a saucepan.) Drain the pasta. Dry the pan.

Spray the pan with oil. Sauté the sausages, onion and green pepper on medium-high heat – stirring often – until the vegetables are tender, about 5 minutes. Stir in the next 5 ingredients. Bring to the boil. Reduce the heat to low and simmer for 10 minutes. Stir in the pasta and coriander. Serve sprinkled with the cheese.

DESSERT SUGGESTION

Maple Kiwifruit Fix

3 each: green and gold kiwifruit
3 tablespoons maple syrup
$^1/_4$ cup walnut pieces, lightly toasted
yoghurt or sorbet to serve

Peel and slice the kiwifruit into a bowl. Drizzle with maple syrup and sprinkle with the walnut pieces. Serve in glasses topped with yoghurt or scoops of sorbet.

Dad's Spaghetti Bolognese

PREPARATION: 10 minutes • COOKING TIME: 50 minutes • SERVES 4

Sauce

3 rashers rindless middle bacon,
    chopped
2 each: large onions, carrots, garlic
    cloves, chopped
600g lean minced beef
400g can diced tomatoes
1 cup beef stock or water
2 tablespoons tomato paste
2 each: bay leaves, sprigs of rosemary,
    oregano and thyme
freshly ground black pepper and salt
    to taste

300g dried or fresh spaghetti

Heat an electric frypan or conventional frying pan. Add the bacon and fry until coloured. Stir in the onions, carrots and garlic, cooking until the onion is softened.

Add the mince. Cook, stirring with a fork to break it up, until the meat has changed colour.

Add the remaining ingredients, except the spaghetti. Cover and simmer for about 45 minutes.

Meanwhile, bring a large saucepan of salted water to the boil. Cook the spaghetti according to the instructions on the packet. Drain.

Serve the meat sauce on top of the spaghetti.

Can be garnished with capers, shredded Parmesan cheese, sliced olives and oregano leaves. Excellent served with a simple green salad on the side.

HINTS

- This sauce can be used as a filling for cannelloni or lasagne.
- Used dried herbs if fresh rosemary, orgeano and thyme are unavailable.

Simple Spinach Salad

350g baby spinach leaves
2 tablespoons each: lemon juice,
    sesame oil
1-2 tablespoons sesame seeds

Wash the spinach leaves in cold water and shake off the excess moisture. Place in a salad bowl.

Just before serving, whisk together the lemon juice and sesame oil and toss with the spinach. Sprinkle with the sesame seeds.

One-pot Seafood Soup

A hearty meal.

PREPARATION: 15 minutes • COOKING TIME: 20 minutes • SERVES 6

1 tablespoon olive oil

2 onions, diced

4 cloves garlic, crushed

1 cup each: dry white wine, fish stock,
    tomato purée

400g can tomatoes in juice, chopped

bunch of fresh mixed herbs, tied with
    string

1 tablespoon sugar

1kg assorted seafood, eg skinned and
    boned white fish fillets, scallops,
    scrubbed mussels in the shell, squid
    rings, prawns

Heat the oil in a deep frying pan and add the onions. Cook on low heat until soft. Stir in the garlic.

Add the wine, fish stock, tomato purée, tomatoes and juice, herbs and sugar. Bring to the boil, reduce the heat and simmer, covered, for 5 minutes.

Cut the fish into 2–3 cm pieces. Add to the soup, bring to the boil, reduce the heat and simmer for 2 minutes. Add the remaining seafood and simmer for a further 2–3 minutes. Remove the herbs and serve immediately in deep bowls with crusty bread.

HINT

To make a good fish stock, place 2 or 3 fish heads in a saucepan, add some herbs and a sliced onion. Cover with water. Slowly bring to the boil. Simmer for about 20 minutes. Cool then strain.

Moroccan Pilaf

PREPARATION: 10 minutes • COOKING TIME: 25 minutes • SERVES 4

2 tablespoons olive oil

1 each: medium onion, carrot, clove
   garlic, diced

1 tablespoon grated root ginger

$^1/_2$ teaspoon each: ground cinnamon,
   coriander, turmeric, chilli paste

1 cup long grain rice

3 cups chicken stock, heated to boiling

$^1/_2$ cup each: currants, quartered dried
   apricots, craisins or raisins, roasted
   unsalted cashew nuts

3 hard-boiled eggs, quartered (optional)

HINTS

- *Craisins are dried cranberries and have a delightfully tangy flavour.*
- *This dish may be frozen and reheated carefully in a frying pan together with a little water or orange juice or in the microwave.*
- *This pilaf also makes an excellent accompaniment for grills or barbecues.*

Heat the oil in an electric frypan or conventional frying pan. Add the onion, carrot, garlic and all the seasonings. Stir well. Cook on low heat for 3–4 minutes.

Add the rice to the pan, stirring to ensure all the grains are coated with oil. Cook for 1 minute.

Add the stock and dried fruits to the rice and bring to the boil. Cover and simmer for about 15 minutes, until the rice is cooked.

Add the cashew nuts, and eggs if using, and heat through.

Excellent garnished with mint leaves and served with steamed asparagus or a crisp green salad.

Vegetarian Mushroom Burgers

PREPARATION 15 minutes • COOKING TIME: 20 minutes • SERVES 4

1 tablespoon rice bran oil
1 large onion, finely diced
2 cloves garlic, crushed
250g flat or brown mushrooms, diced
1 1/2 cups wholegrain breadcrumbs
1 tablespoon lemon juice
2 tablespoons chopped parsley
1 teaspoon each: chopped fresh sage or
*   thyme, soy sauce*
3-4 tablespoons instant polenta

HINTS

- *These burgers are also suitable for cooking on a barbecue hotplate.*
- *Polenta is a maize ground into cornmeal. It is great for preventing burgers and patties from sticking to a frying pan. If polenta is unavailable, use dry breadcrumbs.*

Heat the oil in an electric frypan. Sauté the onion and garlic until the onion is soft. Add the mushrooms and cook until soft and all the liquid has evaporated. Add the breadcrumbs, lemon juice, herbs and soy sauce.

Divide into 4 portions and mould into patties. Dust with polenta.

Pan-fry over medium heat for about 3-4 minutes on each side.

Great served in baps with a little mustard, some mayo, and salad ingredients.

DESSERT SUGGESTION

Frozen Berry Ice Cream

2 cups frozen berries
1 cup cream

Place the berries in a blender. With the motor running, slowly add the cream. Continue mixing until fairly smooth. This may need to be done in batches. Best enjoyed immediately.

Asparagus & Pea Risotto

Broccoli florets also make a good addition to this recipe.

PREPARATION: 10 minutes • COOKING TIME: 30 minutes • SERVES 4-5

3 tablespoons olive oil
1 each: onion, carrot, diced
2 cloves garlic, crushed
1^1/2 cups Arborio risotto rice
5^1/2 cups boiling vegetable
  or chicken stock
250g fresh asparagus, trimmed
1 cup fresh or frozen peas
^{1}/4 cup finely grated Parmesan cheese
freshly ground black pepper to taste

Heat 2 tablespoons of the oil in an electric frypan or large frying pan over medium heat. Add the onion and carrot and sauté for 5 minutes. Add the garlic and sauté for 30 seconds. Stir in the rice and cook until the grains are shiny, about 1 minute.

Add ^{1}/2 cup of stock to the rice and bring to the boil, stirring constantly. Cook the rice briskly, stirring constantly, until most of the liquid is absorbed. Repeat using ^{1}/2 cup of stock each time, cooking until the rice is just tender but the mixture is still slightly runny.

Meanwhile, slice the asparagus diagonally. Add to the risotto with the peas. Cook until just tender. Stir in half the Parmesan cheese.

Serve in shallow bowls topped with the remaining Parmesan and black pepper.

HINTS

- *Bring the stock to the boil in a saucepan or in the microwave.*
- *Arborio or risotto rice can absorb large amounts of liquid while remaining firm.*
- *Ask the children to grate the cheese.*

Cheesy Quesadillas & Kiwifruit Salsa

PREPARATION: 10 minutes • COOKING TIME: 20 minutes • SERVES 4 as a light meal

Kiwifruit Salsa

1 cup finely diced kiwifruit
1 teaspoon chilli paste
3 tablespoons each: chopped coriander
* leaves, mint leaves*
2 spring onions, diced
3-4 tablespoons lime or lemon juice
freshly ground salt and pepper to taste

12 flour tortillas
4 1/2 cups grated cheddar cheese
2 each: small green and red peppers
* (capsicum), seeded and diced*
spray oil

HINTS

- *Flour tortillas are readily available from your supermarket.*
- *Quesadilla (a form of sandwich) is pronounced kay-sa-dee-ya.*
- *Pawpaw or tomatoes could replace the kiwifruit in the salsa.*
- *Diced onion or chopped sautéed bacon could be added to the quesadilla filling.*

To make the salsa combine all of the ingredients, tossing gently to mix.

To make the quesadillas, sprinkle 6 flour tortillas with equal portions of cheese and peppers. Top each with the remaining tortillas.

Spray a large electric frypan with oil.

Cook the quesadillas on medium heat, turning once or twice, until the cheese is melted. Remove from the frypan. Cut each quesadilla into 4 or 8 wedges and serve immediately with the salsa and a salad.

Butter Chicken with Veggies

1 onion, sliced

1 tablespoon rice bran or other
    vegetable oil

1 kumara, peeled and cubed

2 cups broccoli florets (1 head)

50g packet butter chicken spice paste

1 tablespoon tomato paste

6 mushrooms, sliced

2 cups sliced, cooked chicken

400g can lite coconut milk

HINTS

- *Yoghurt could replace the coconut milk.*
- *Other vegetables could be added.*
- *Serve garnished with herbs such as parsley, coriander or basil.*

Sauté the onion in the oil in a non-stick frying pan until softened. Add the kumara, stir well, then cover and continue cooking for about 15 minutes until the kumara is softened. Meanwhile, cut the broccoli into florets. Peel and slice the broccoli stem.

Stir the spice paste and tomato paste into the pan. Add the mushrooms. Stir well and heat for 1 minute. Add the chicken, coconut milk and broccoli. Stir well, then simmer until heated through.

Serve in bowls with rice or naan bread.

Egg Fried Rice with Cashews

Cook the rice the day before to allow it to become dry enough for pan-frying. Or use rice that has been frozen and then thawed.

400g lean boneless pork or skinned and boned chicken thighs

1 tablespoon each: orange juice, soy sauce, cornflour

1 teaspoon sugar

oil for frying

2 eggs, lightly beaten

4 cups cooked long grain rice (about 1^1/2 cups raw)

^{1}/2 cup toasted cashew nuts

1 spring onion, diagonally sliced

HINTS

- *When cooking rice for meals, cook double the quantity required. Drain, cool and freeze the leftover rice in an airtight container for up to 6 months. It can be quickly thawed in the microwave or over boiling water and used as an accompaniment or in pan-fries.*
- *Diced vegetables could be added to the rice.*
- *Serve with chilli on the side if preferred.*

Cut the meat into very thin pieces. Mix the orange juice, soy sauce, cornflour and sugar. Add the meat to this mixture, mixing until well coated.

Heat 2 teaspoons of oil in a frying pan on low, then add the eggs. Swirl the eggs in the pan and cook until set. Transfer to a board, roll up, and cut into thin rounds.

Heat 1 tablespoon of oil in an electric frypan and stir-fry the meat until cooked, about 2-3 minutes. Transfer to a plate.

Add another 2 teaspoons of oil to the pan and add the rice. Stir-fry for 2 minutes until all the grains are separated.

Add the cooked meat, nuts, egg and spring onion and cook for just long enough to heat through. Serve immediately.

GROOVY
GRILLS

Moroccan Marinated Grilled Pork

PREPARATION: 15 minutes (plus refrigeration time), at least 1 hour
COOKING TIME: 10 minutes • SERVES 4

Moroccan Marinade

$1/2$ cup wine vinegar or balsamic vinegar
2 tablespoons each: tomato paste,
   honey
1 teaspoon each: ground coriander,
   cumin, turmeric, ginger
$1/4$ cup olive oil

600g lean pork fillet or steak

wooden skewers (soaked in warm water
   for 30 minutes)

Combine all the ingredients for the marinade in a small bowl or ceramic dish.

Cut the pork into 2.5cm cubes. Thread onto skewers. Brush well with the marinade. Cover and refrigerate for at least 1 hour.

Preheat the grill (see Hints below). Cook the pork for about 3-5 minutes on each side, brushing well with the remaining marinade.

Great served with an orange and baby spinach salad.

HINTS

- *This marinade is also suitable for fish, lamb or chicken.*
- *Most oven grills need to be preheated before cooking commences. Turn the temperature to about 220°C or slightly above, depending on the type of food. Beef and lamb steaks are usually grilled at a higher temperature than chicken or fish or very thick cuts of red meat.*
- *The food to be cooked should be placed on a sturdy grilling rack about 6-7cm below the heat source. With most ovens, the door is left open during cooking to ensure there is sufficient ventilation. Lightly oil or grease a preheated grilling rack to prevent sticking.*
- *Turbo grilling – where the cooking is enhanced by the oven fan – is available in some ovens. This method is very efficient and requires the oven door to be closed during cooking. Always follow the manufacturer's instructions.*

Franks 'n Bacon

PREPARATION: 5 minutes • COOKING TIME: 8 minutes • Makes 8

8 each: medium frankfurters, streaky
   bacon rashers
1/2 cup Thai-style sweet chilli sauce
8 each: long rolls, large lettuce leaves
4 tomatoes, sliced
1 small cucumber, sliced
mustard sauce to taste

DESSERT SUGGESTION

Hot Blueberry Sauce
*A delicious topping for ice cream,
pancakes or waffles.*

1/3 cup sugar
1*1/2* tablespoons plain flour
1 tablespoon lemon juice
1/2 cup each: water, good red wine (or
   cranberry juice)
1 cup fresh or frozen blueberries
1 tablespooon butter, chopped
2 tablespoons orange-flavoured liqueur
   (optional)

Combine the sugar and flour in a heavy
saucepan. Slowly whisk in the lemon juice,
water and wine. Stir over low heat until
smooth.

Add the blueberries and cook gently,
stirring, until thickened. Remove from the
heat and add the butter and liqueur. Serve
hot or warm.

*Makes about 1*1/2* cups*

Insert a long skewer into each frankfurter. Wrap a rasher of bacon along each frank. Brush with chilli sauce.

Cook under a preheated medium-high grill for about 3-4 minutes on each side or until cooked.

Slide the cooked franks into long rolls, split lengthways and lined with lettuce leaves.

Add the sliced tomato, cucumber and mustard sauce.

Lamb Kebabs with Tapenade Dressing

PREPARATION: 10 minutes (plus 2-3 hours marinating time)
COOKING TIME: 10 minutes • SERVES 4

4 large, thick lamb leg steaks
2-3 tablespoons olive oil
salt and freshly ground black pepper
4 cloves garlic, crushed
1/4 cup each: chopped thyme, rosemary

Tapenade Dressing

3 tablespoons each: prepared tapenade,
* mayonnaise*
1 tablespoon lemon juice
freshly ground black pepper to taste

HINTS

- *Tapenade (minced black olives, olive oil and seasonings) is available at most supermarkets.*
- *Choose tender cuts of meat for grilling and ensure that they are at room temperature prior to cooking otherwise the outside may be cooked – or even charred – long before the inside.*
- *Any fat or skin around the edges of the meat should be snipped at 3cm intervals to prevent it curling out of shape during cooking.*
- *Ensure that meat coated with marinades containing sugar or honey are cooked at a lower temperature or further away from the grill to prevent scorching.*
- *Tenting the meat with foil for up to 10 minutes after removing from the oven allows the meat to 'set' and makes it easier to carve.*

Cut the lamb into cubes and thread the meat pieces onto skewers.

Brush with the oil, then sprinkle with the salt, pepper, garlic and herbs, pressing in well. Cover and refrigerate for several hours.

Bring the meat up to room temperature and place on a grilling rack. Drizzle with a little oil. Cook under a preheated grill on high for about 4-5 minutes on each side. Stand tented in foil for 3-4 minutes before serving.

Meanwhile, combine the ingredients for the dressing. Serve with the lamb.

Excellent served with vegetables that have been cut into 2.5cm squares, sprayed with oil, sprinkled with black pepper and grilled at the same time.

Fan-grilled Crunchy Fish

PREPARATION: 5 minutes • COOKING TIME: 8 minutes • SERVES 4

spray oil
600g skinned and boned thick
    fish fillets
4 tablespoons basil pesto
3/4 cup breadcrumbs
salt and pepper to taste

HINTS

- *Fish is often best grilled on a flat oven tray or in a shallow roasting dish about 15cm from the source of heat, depending on whether or not you can adjust the grill temperature.*
- *Fan (turbo) grilling is carried out with the door closed.*

DESSERT SUGGESTION

Grilled Fruit Kebabs

1 large banana
2 firm but ripe kiwifruit
4 pineapple rings
25g butter, melted
2 tablespoons brown sugar

Peel and cut the banana into 2.5cm pieces. Peel and thickly slice the kiwifruit. Quarter the pineapple rings. Thread the fruit alternately onto skewers.

Brush with the butter and sprinkle with sugar. Grill until lightly coloured and warm. Serve with yoghurt.

Preheat the grill to 180°C. Lightly spray an oven tray or rack with oil.

Divide the fish into 4 equal pieces. Brush all over with the pesto.

Combine the breadcrumbs, salt and pepper.

Dip the fish in the breadcrumbs to coat well. Place on the oven tray or rack. Lightly spray the fish with oil.

Place the tray with the fish just above the middle of the oven and fan grill (with the door closed) for 3-4 minutes. Turn the pieces over, dusting with a few more crumbs if necessary and lightly spray with oil again. Continue grilling for about 4 minutes or until the fish is cooked.

Great served with grilled tomatoes, potato mash and steamed broccoli.

Mexican Beef

PREPARATION: 5 minutes (plus 2-3 hours marinating time)
COOKING TIME: 8 minutes (plus resting time) • SERVES 4-6

3 tablespoons canola or other
vegetable oil
1 tablespoon paprika
1-2 teaspoons chilli powder
1 teaspoon ground cumin
1kg rump steak in the piece, cut 3cm
thick

Spuds USA

16 small potatoes
25g butter or margarine, softened
3 tablespoons each: coarsely ground
salt, black pepper
1 tablespoon chilli flakes

wooden skewers (soaked in warm water
for 30 minutes)

Steam or microwave the potatoes until just tender. Cool.

Thread onto skewers. Brush well with the butter. Sprinkle with the salt, pepper and chilli flakes. Grill until golden brown.

Combine the oil, paprika, chilli powder and cumin. Spread over both sides of the steak. Marinate for several hours or overnight in the refrigerator.

Preheat the grill. Cook the beef for about 3-4 minutes on each side, until cooked to taste. Rest – tented in foil to retain heat – for 2-3 minutes. Cut into 1cm-thick slices across the grain.

Super served with a tomato salsa, a green salad and/or avocado and Spuds USA.

Barbecue-style Chicken

PREPARATION: 5 minutes (plus 8 hours marinating time)
COOKING TIME: 12 minutes • SERVES 4

8 skinned and boned chicken thighs

Marinade
$1/2$ cup tomato purée
*1 tablespoon each: Worcestershire
    sauce, lemon juice, prepared mustard*
*1 teaspoon each: sugar, mixed dried
    herbs*

HINT
*Place wooden (bamboo) skewers in warm
water and soak for at least 30 minutes
before using to avoid burning.*

Smashed Peas & Potatoes
3 medium potatoes, peeled and chopped
2 cups frozen peas
2 cloves garlic, crushed (optional)
salt and pepper to taste
2 tablespoons olive oil

Boil the potatoes until just cooked. Add
the peas and continue cooking until the
peas are hot. Drain. Season with the garlic,
salt and pepper. Add the oil and mash well.

Place the chicken thighs in a plastic bag. Add the
combined marinade ingredients and refrigerate for up
to 8 hours. Drain.

If preferred, insert wooden skewers diagonally through
each thigh to hold in shape. Place on a grilling rack.

Preheat the grill.

Cook the chicken under the medium-high grill for about
12 minutes or until cooked, turning and basting often.

Pita Burgers

PREPARATION: 15 minutes • COOKING TIME: 10 minutes • SERVES 4

500g lean minced lamb or beef
grated rind of $^1/_2$ lemon
2 tablespoons each: lemon juice, finely
   chopped parsley
2 cloves garlic, crushed
freshly ground salt and pepper to taste
6 large stuffed green olives, finely
   chopped
4 medium pita breads
salad ingredients of choice

Combine the mince with the rest of the ingredients
except the pita breads and salad. Shape into 8 patties
each about 1cm thick. Refrigerate until ready to cook.

Preheat the grill. Cook the patties under medium heat
for about 4 minutes on each side.

Meanwhile, halve the pita breads. Wrap them in paper
towels and warm through for 1-2 minutes in the
microwave or steam, wrapped in foil over boiling water.
Warming the pitas makes them easier to fill.

Fill the pita halves with the salad ingredients and the
patties.

Great topped with a dollop of yoghurt and/or basil
pesto.

Basil Pesto

1 $^1/_2$ cups packed basil leaves
3 cloves garlic
$^1/_3$ cup lightly toasted pine nuts, macadamia nuts or walnuts,
   chopped
$^1/_2$ cup extra virgin olive oil
$^1/_2$ cup grated Parmesan cheese
salt and freshly ground black pepper to taste

Place the basil, garlic, nuts and a little olive oil in a blender or
food processor and process until coarsely chopped. With the
motor running, slowly drizzle in the remaining olive oil. Fold
in the Parmesan cheese and seasonings.

Makes about 1 cup

Cutlets with Cheese Crumble

PREPARATION: 15 minutes • COOKING TIME: 8 minutes • SERVES 4

1 cup fresh breadcrumbs
100g tasty cheddar cheese or cumin
seed cheese, grated
$^1/_4$ cup chopped parsley
salt and pepper to taste
12 lamb cutlets

HINTS

Asian greens add interest to meals.

- *Chinese cabbage (wong bok) is a large, firm cabbage with long, pale green leaves and white stems. Crisp and crunchy, wong bok is excellent in salads and quick stir-fries.*
- *Bok choy (pak choy) has long white stems and smooth green leaves. Because they are a little tough they are best steamed or stir-fried.*
- *Shanghai cabbage is baby bok choy (pak choy) – a smaller cabbage with thick, crisp, tender, juicy white stems and smooth green leaves. Steam whole or slice for stir-fries or use raw – sliced – in salads.*
- *Choy sum – a flowering Chinese cabbage with long, thin, green stems, small, light-green leaves and yellow flowers – is great for stir-fries or steaming or in salads.*
- *Gai lan is similar in appearance to choy sum but has white flowers and darker green leaves. The stems can be tough so cook this vegetable either by steaming or stir-frying.*

Combine the breadcrumbs, cheese, parsley and seasonings. Preheat the grill to high.

Place the cutlets on a grilling rack and grill for 3 minutes on one side.

Turn the cutlets over and place equal portions of the crumble mixture on each one. Grill for a further 3-4 minutes until cooked and the topping is golden.

Great served with steamed bok choy or Shanghai cabbage and steamed or sautéed potatoes.

Chiang Mai Chicken Patties

PREPARATION: 10 minutes (plus 30 minutes refrigeration time)
COOKING TIME: 6 minutes • SERVES 4

500g minced chicken
2 tablespoons Thai red curry paste
finely grated rind of 1 lime or lemon
1 egg, lightly beaten
1-2 teaspoons fish sauce

HINTS

- *When forming meatballs or patties, roll each portion of the meat in your palms for 30 seconds, then shape. The rolling helps the meat stick together during cooking.*
- *Fish sauce is a thin, salty, light brown sauce used in South-East Asian cooking. If preferred, substitute light soy sauce.*

Combine all the ingredients in a bowl. Form the mixture into small patties each about 5cm in diameter. Refrigerate for 30 minutes.

Preheat the grill to medium-high. Cook the patties for about 3 minutes on each side or until cooked through.

Excellent served on a plate of crisp lettuce leaves and garnished with fresh herbs. Serve with rice and dipping sauces such as sweet Thai chilli sauce or sweet and sour sauce.

Koftas with Hummus

2 slices bread, crusts removed
1 egg, beaten
500g minced lamb or beef
1 onion, grated
1 clove garlic, crushed
1 teaspoon each: ground cumin,
*   coriander*
2 tablespoons chopped parsley
$^3/_4$ cup hummus
4 large lettuce leaves, sliced

Soak the bread in the beaten egg. Place all the ingredients except the hummus and lettuce in a food processor and blend well. Shape heaped tablespoons of the mixture into balls. Refrigerate for 1-2 hours, if possible.

Preheat the grill to medium-high. Place the koftas on a grilling pan. Grill for about 6 minutes until cooked, turning occasionally.

Excellent served topped with hummus in lettuce-lined pita pockets or on rice with cucumber, tomatoes, and yoghurt as accompaniments.

Hummus

390g can cooked chick peas (also called garbanzos)
2 tablespoons tahini
2 cloves garlic, crushed
$^1/_2$ teaspoon each: ground cumin, chilli paste
salt, pepper and lemon juice to taste
2 tablespoons extra virgin olive oil

Drain the chick peas and place in a food processor or blender. Add all the other ingredients except the oil. Blend until smooth. Place in a bowl and pour the olive oil over.

Use as a topping for koftas, roast lamb, kebabs, burgers or as a dip for crispy veggies.

Makes about 1 cup

Potato Wedges with Red Pepper & Cheddar

PREPARATION: 15 minutes • COOKING TIME: 10 minutes • SERVES 4

4 medium baking potatoes, cut into
   thick wedges
1 red pepper (capsicum)
3 spring onions
salt and pepper to taste
$^1/_2$ teaspoon smoked paprika
$^3/_4$ cup lite cream cheese
$^1/_4$ cup milk
$^1/_2$ cup grated tasty cheddar cheese

Rocket & Asparagus Salad

12 stalks asparagus
3 cups rocket leaves
8 each: cherry tomatoes, pitted black
   olives
$^1/_2$ cup balsamic dressing (readily available
   from your supermarket)

Trim the asparagus then blanch (place in boiling water briefly) until crisp-tender. Refresh in cold water. Drain and pat dry.

Arrange the asparagus on a serving plate with the rocket, halved cherry tomatoes and black olives. Drizzle with the dressing.

Steam or microwave the potato wedges until just tender.

Meanwhile, seed and thinly slice the red pepper and chop the spring onions.

Drain the potatoes well. Combine with the red pepper and spring onions in a heatproof dish. Season well and sprinkle with the paprika.

Preheat the grill to high.

Whisk together the cream cheese and milk, then pour over the potato mixture. Sprinkle with the cheese.

Grill for 5-10 minutes until the vegetables are hot and the cheese has melted.

Excellent served with a green salad and/or grilled tomatoes.

Grilled Vegetables with Chermoula

PREPARATION: 20 minutes • COOKING TIME: 10 minutes • SERVES 4-6

Chermoula

1 small red onion, finely diced
3 cloves garlic, crushed
1 teaspoon each: ground cumin, paprika
pinch each: cayenne, salt
$^1/_2$ cup each: chopped parsley, coriander,
    extra virgin olive oil
3 tablespoons lemon juice

Vegetables

1 each: red pepper, green pepper
    (capsicum)
1 small eggplant, cut into 2cm-thick
    rounds
1 large red onion, cut into 2cm-thick
    rounds
1 large courgette, quartered lengthways
4 mushrooms
1 large carrot, cut diagonally into
    5mm-thick slices
salt and pepper to taste

spray oil
freshly ground black pepper to taste

HINTS

- *The sliced eggplant can be sprinkled with a teaspoon of salt and left to stand for 30 minutes. This helps to eliminate any bitter flavours and softens the eggplant. Rinse and pat dry before cooking.*
- *Add protein by grilling slices of feta with the vegetables.*

Combine the ingredients for the Chermoula and mix well.

Quarter the peppers lengthways and remove the seeds. Place the vegetables on a shallow oven tray. Spray with the oil and season.

Preheat the grill to high. Cook the veggies for about 4 minutes on each side or until cooked and golden. Serve topped with Chermoula. Excellent served with crusty bread. (Chermoula is also an excellent topping for lamb or potatoes.)

SNAPPY
STIR-FRIES

Quick Thai-style Veggie Curry

PREPARATION: 15 minutes • COOKING TIME: 20 minutes • SERVES 4

1 tablespoon canola or other
   vegetable oil
1 each: red onion, clove garlic, diced
1-2 tablespoons Thai red curry paste
250g each: cauliflorets, frozen beans,
   peeled and diced pumpkin
$^1/_4$ cup water
$^3/_4$ cup plain yoghurt or coconut cream
2 teaspoons flour (preferably
   wholemeal)
salt and pepper to taste

Heat the oil in a large heavy saucepan or wok. Sauté the onion and garlic until soft. Stir in the curry paste.

Add the vegetables and stir-fry for 5 minutes. Add the water and simmer for another 5 minutes or until the veggies are crisp-tender. Stir in the yoghurt mixed with the flour. Heat through. Season.

Great garnished with fresh herbs such as mint or coriander and served with rice.

HINTS

- *For extra flavour, add grated lemon rind or a finely chopped young lemon leaf to the rice while cooking.*
- *Thai-style curry pastes are readily available in packets or jars from your supermarket. Use according to your own taste.*
- *Prior to cooking, heat the saucepan or wok for a couple of minutes before adding the oil. Begin cooking the most dense foods (eg carrot) first, adding a little at a time, stir-frying continuously so they don't 'stew'.*
- *Vegetables can often take longer to cook than meats so cook them first, remove from the pan then cook the meat. Return the vegetables to heat through.*
- *Stir-frying is not limited to Asian recipes. Combos of Mediterranean foods are often stir-fried and served with pasta.*
- *If you're weight-watching, stir-fry meat and veggies in water or fruit juice rather than oil. The flavour isn't the same but the lack of calories may compensate.*

Hoisin Chicken in Lettuce Cups

PREPARATION: 15 minutes • COOKING TIME: 10 minutes • SERVES 4

2 tablespoons canola or other
   vegetable oil
1 tablespoon grated root ginger
$^1/_4$ teaspoon salt
2 spring onions, finely chopped
500g minced chicken
125g can sliced water chestnuts, rinsed
   and coarsely chopped
$^1/_4$ cup hoisin sauce
1 teaspoon each: chilli sauce, rice
   vinegar
12 large, crisp iceberg lettuce leaves

HINT

*Hoisin sauce, readily availablefrom your
supermarket, contains soy bean paste,
garlic, vinegar and various spices. For first-
time users, a little water can be added to
make the flavour less strong.*

Heat a wok or large, heavy frying pan over moderately
high heat. Add the oil.

Stir in the ginger, salt and half the spring onions. Stir-
fry until the ginger is fragrant, about 45 seconds.

Add the chicken and stir-fry until cooked through, about
5 minutes. Add the water chestnuts, hoisin sauce, chilli
sauce and vinegar. Stir-fry until heated through, about
2 minutes.

Transfer to a bowl and sprinkle with the remaining
spring onions.

The idea is that everyone serves themselves by
spooning the chicken mixture into the lettuce leaves
and wrapping the leaves around the filling to enclose.

Serve with boiled rice and diced salad veggies, eg
tomatoes, cucumber and red onion.

Gnocchi Stir-fry with Courgettes & Ricotta

PREPARATION: 5 minutes • COOKING TIME: 15 minutes • SERVES 4

400g potato gnocchi
25g butter
1 tablespoon olive oil
3 courgettes, sliced
200g ricotta cheese
1 clove garlic, crushed
2 tablespoons oregano leaves
salt and pepper to taste
50g shaved Parmesan cheese

Tomato & Caper Salad

4 anchovies (optional)
8 medium vine-ripened tomatoes
2 large shallots, sliced and rinsed in cold
    water
2 tablespoons capers, rinsed and drained
salt and freshly ground black pepper to
    taste
1/4 cup extra virgin olive oil
1 tablespoon each: lemon juice, chopped
    parsley
1 teaspoon thyme leaves

If using anchovies, soak in water or milk to remove some of the salt. Rinse and pat dry.

Core the tomatoes. Thickly slice. Place on a serving plate. Top with the shallots, anchovies and capers. Season to taste.

Combine the olive oil, lemon juice, parsley and thyme and drizzle over the tomatoes.

Cook the gnocchi in boiling salted water until floating and very tender. Remove and refresh in cold water. Drain well.

Heat the butter and oil together in a large wok or heavy frying pan.

Add the courgettes and stir-fry for 2 minutes. Remove from the pan and place to one side. Add the gnocchi and stir until they start to turn golden.

Add the ricotta, garlic, oregano and cooked courgettes. Cook for 2 minutes. Add about 1 tablespoon of water if the mixture is too dry. Season. Serve topped with the Parmesan cheese.

Great served with a tomato salad.

HINT

Gnocchi, readily available (and usually vacuum-packed) from your supermarket, are small Italian dumplings traditionally made from potato.

Pork & Apple Stir-fry

PREPARATION: 10 minutes (plus 1 hour marinating time)
COOKING TIME: 15 minutes • SERVES 4

500g Trim Pork schnitzels
$^1/_2$ cup apple juice
1 tablespoon each: honey, finely grated
    root ginger
1 large apple
2 stalks celery, thinly sliced
$^1/_2$ cup each: whole kernel corn, sultanas
freshly ground black pepper to taste
3 cups finely shredded cabbage
1 teaspoon cornflour

HINT

For best results when stir-frying, prepare all the ingredients ahead of time. Cut foods into thin strips or pieces of about equal size. This applies especially to vegetables that are fairly dense in texture such as carrots, cauliflower and beans. These could be blanched prior to stir-frying either briefly in boiling water or in the microwave.

Cut the meat into 2cm-wide strips. Combine with the apple juice, honey and ginger. Marinate for 1 hour.

Meanwhile, core and thinly slice the apple.

Drain the meat, reserving the marinade. Pat dry with a paper towel. Sauté the meat for 2-3 minutes in a hot, non-stick wok or frying pan.

Add the apple, celery, corn, sultanas and black pepper. Stir-fry for about 5 minutes until the vegetables are crisp-tender. Add the cabbage and stir-fry for 1 minute.

Combine the cornflour with the reserved marinade and stir into the pork mixture. Cook until thickened.

Excellent served with noodles or rice.

Mediterranean Stir-fry

PREPARATION: 15 minutes (not including the salting time)
COOKING TIME: 10 minutes • SERVES 4

1 small eggplant
1 teaspoon salt
1 each: red, green and yellow pepper
   (capsicum)
2 courgettes
3-4 tablespoons olive oil
2 cloves garlic, crushed
150g feta cheese, chopped
1 tablespoon chopped mixed herbs, eg
   rosemary, thyme, oregano
basil leaves to garnish

Cut the eggplant into 5mm-thick rounds and cut each round in half. Sprinkle with the salt and stand for 30 minutes. This removes any bitterness from the eggplant. Drain, wash and pat dry.

Halve, seed and slice the peppers into 1cm strips. Cut the courgettes into 1cm rounds.

Heat the oil in a large heavy wok or frying pan and add the garlic. Add the eggplant and stir-fry for 1 minute until softened. Add the remaining vegetables in batches and stir-fry until just tender. Add the feta and mixed herbs. Stir-fry for 1 minute. Garnish with basil leaves.

May be served with pasta or rice.

HINTS

- *Olive oils from different countries vary in character. Italian oil has a nutty taste, Greek olive oil is usually thick and Spanish oil has a full flavour.*
- *The most expensive olive oil is 'extra virgin'. Extracted from the first cold pressing of the olives, it is usually greenish in colour, sometimes helped by the addition of a few leaves to the press. It is ideal for salads and mayonnaise where its true flavour can be appreciated.*
- *Cold-pressed oils retain their vitamin A and E content better than those extracted by heat.*
- *Further pressings of the olives produce oils with milder flavours and paler colours They can be less expensive and are best suited for cooking.*

DESSERT SUGGESTION

Quick Strawberry Trifle
100g trifle sponge or similar
$1/4$ cup orange-flavoured liqueur or orange juice
$1/2$ cup cream
1 tablespoon icing sugar
2-3 cups strawberries, washed and hulled

Break up the trifle sponge with your fingers and place in 4 serving bowls. Drizzle with the liqueur or orange juice.

Whip together the cream and icing sugar, until soft peaks form. Crush $1/2$ cup of strawberries and combine with the cream. Slice the remaining strawberries. Place on top of the sponge and top with the strawberry cream.

Tropical Chicken Salad

PREPARATION: 10 minutes (plus 30 minutes marinating time)
COOKING TIME: 5 minutes • SERVES 4

*400g chicken tenderloins or skinned
and boned chicken breasts*
$^1/_2$ cup pineapple juice
1 teaspoon sesame oil
1 tablespoon olive oil
$1^1/_2$ cups sliced pawpaw or peaches
3-4 cups assorted salad greens
$^1/_4$ cup vinaigrette
freshly ground black pepper to taste

Red Wine Vinaigrette

$^1/_2$ cup red wine vinegar
1 large shallot, diced
2 cloves garlic, crushed
*1 tablespoon each: chopped thyme,
rosemary, marjoram*
*freshly ground salt and black pepper to
taste*
1 cup extra virgin olive oil
2 teaspoons Dijon-style mustard

Whisk together the vinegar, shallot, garlic, herbs, salt and pepper until well combined. Cover and refrigerate for about 8 hours. Strain through a sieve.

Whisk the oil and mustard into the strained vinegar. Cover and refrigerate for up to 1 week.

Makes about $1^1/_2$ cups

If using chicken breasts, slice each one lengthways into 3 pieces.

Place the chicken in a shallow dish and add the combined pineapple juice and sesame oil. Marinate for at least 30 minutes in the refrigerator. Drain and pat dry with a paper towel.

Heat the olive oil in a non-stick frying pan. Add the chicken and stir-fry for 2–3 minutes until coloured on the outside. Remove to one side. Add the sliced fruit and stir-fry for 1 minute. Slice the cooked chicken into 3cm pieces and return to the pan. Add the marinade and heat through for no more than 1 minute.

Toss the salad greens lightly with the vinaigrette and pile on 4 serving plates. Top with the chicken and fruit. Sprinkle with black pepper.

Ma Shu Burrito

A fusion of Chinese and Mexican.

PREPARATION: 15 minutes • COOKING TIME: 10 minutes • SERVES 4

3 tablespoons each: soy sauce, water
1 tablespoon each: brown sugar,
   grated root ginger
1 each: medium onion, green
   pepper (capsicum), sliced
$1^1/_2$ cups sliced mushrooms
$^1/_2$ cup mung bean sprouts
2 tablespoons peanut oil
2 cups cooked, minced pork
4 tablespoons hoisin sauce
4 medium flour tortillas, warmed

HINTS

- *A great recipe for using leftover cooked meats.*
- *Cooked chicken could replace the pork.*
- *Warm the tortillas in the microwave for about 1 minute. Alternatively, wrap in foil and heat over boiling water.*

Combine the soy sauce, water, sugar and ginger in a bowl and set aside.

Prepare the vegetables and set aside in separate piles.

Heat the oil in a wok or large frying pan and stir-fry the onion and pepper for about 3 minutes. Add the mushrooms and cook for 2 minutes. Add the bean sprouts and pork, then pour in the soy mixture. Cook over medium heat, tossing constantly until the liquid evaporates.

Spread the hoisin sauce over the tortillas. Spoon the filling over to about 2cm from the edge of each tortilla. Fold the bottom edge up and the outside edges in to enclose the filling. Serve immediately.

Pad Thai

250g rice stick noodles
3 tablespoons canola or other
  vegetable oil
1 large onion, diced
24 large raw prawns
1 tablespoon each: chopped garlic,
  chilli paste
2 tablespoons each: palm or brown
  sugar, tamarind paste, fish sauce
2 cups mung bean sprouts
$^1/_2$ cup roasted peanuts, chopped
4 eggs, lightly beaten

Boil the noodles in water until soft, about 2–3 minutes. Drain and mix with a little oil.

Heat half the remaining oil in a wok or large frying pan and stir-fry the onion for 1 minute. Add the prawns and garlic and cook until the prawns are just pink. Remove from the heat.

Add the chilli paste, sugar, tamarind paste, fish sauce, cooked noodles, bean sprouts and peanuts.

Return to the heat. Add the eggs, toss briefly and heat until warmed through.

HINTS

- *Chilli paste is sometimes called sambal oeleck. It is a mixture of diced chillies, salt and vinegar. Some chilli pastes are hot and harsh and some are soft and mellow. Use according to your taste.*
- *Tamarind is an acid-tasting fruit which is sold dried, in packets. Soak a 5cm piece in a cup of water for 10 minutes, then squeeze it until it mixes with the water. Strain out the seeds and fibre before using the liquid. Ready-to-use tamarind paste is now available. Lemon or lime juice could replace the tamarind liquid.*
- *Palm sugar is strong-flavoured brown sugar obtained from coconut palms. Brown sugar is an acceptable substitute.*

DESSERT SUGGESTION

Poached Strawberries & Rhubarb

4 cups hulled and sliced strawberries
$^1/_4$ cup sugar
1 tablespoon lemon juice
cold water
2 tablespoons cornflour
$1^1/_2$ cups finely diced rhubarb

Sprinkle the strawberries with 2 tablespoons of the sugar and the lemon juice. Toss carefully. Stand for 30 minutes. Strain, reserving the strawberries and juice separately. Add enough cold water to the juice to make $^3/_4$ of a cup.

Combine the remaining sugar and cornflour in a saucepan. Stir in the reserved juice, rhubarb and $^1/_2$ cup of strawberries. Simmer, stirring occasionally, until the rhubarb is cooked.

Cool to room temperature. Fold in the remaining strawberries. Spoon into serving dishes or glasses. Refrigerate to chill. Great served with yoghurt or whipped cream.

Stir-fried Summer Veggies & Spaghetti

PREPARATION: 15 minutes • COOKING TIME: 20 minutes • SERVES 4

300g dried spaghetti
2 tablespoons olive oil
1 onion, diced
1 each: large green and red pepper
  (capsicum), garlic clove
4 medium tomatoes
2 tablespoons lemon juice
6 pitted black olives, sliced
1 avocado, peeled, stoned and diced
freshly ground black pepper and grated
  Parmesan cheese to taste

HINTS

* *For variation, add a can of drained flaked salmon; crumbled feta cheese; grilled diced bacon; or diced smoked chicken.*
* *Choose about 300g of dried pasta or 400g of fresh to serve 4 people.*

Boil the spaghetti according to the instructions on the packet.

Meanwhile, heat the olive oil in a large, preferably non-stick, frying pan. Stir-fry the onion until softened.

Halve, seed and dice the peppers. Crush the garlic. Core the tomatoes and cut each one into 8 wedges.

Add the peppers to the pan and stir-fry for 1 minute. Add the garlic and tomatoes and stir-fry until the tomatoes are slightly softened. Stir in the lemon juice, olives, avocado, black pepper and Parmesan cheese.

Drain the spaghetti and place in a large serving bowl. Toss the vegetable mixture with the spaghetti. Serve immediately.

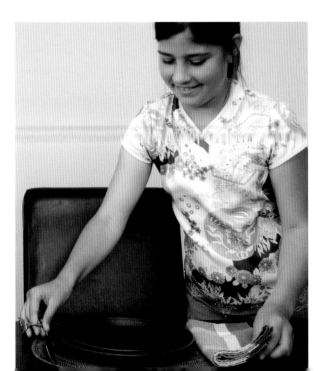

Mussels with Lemon

PREPARATION: 15 minutes • COOKING TIME: 10 minutes • SERVES 4

1kg mussels in the shell (about 40)
1 lemon
1 medium onion, diced
1 tablespoon canola or other
  vegetable oil
2 cloves garlic, crushed
1 teaspoon chilli paste
$^1/_2$ cup water
chopped parsley to garnish

HINTS

- *To julienne vegetables, fruits and other foods is to cut them into very thin sticks.*
- *After purchasing fresh seafood, store in the refrigerator as quickly as possible. Before refrigerating, take it out of the wrapping and place in a single layer on a flat dish. Cover with plastic film and make 2-3 little holes in the plastic to allow some air circulation. Alternatively, cover loosely in waxed paper. Use seafood as soon as possible after purchasing.*

Wash the mussels well in cold water. Discard any that float or refuse to close when given a sharp tap. Scrub the mussels and cut off the beards with scissors.

Thinly peel the lemon. Julienne the rind. Squeeze the juice and place to one side. Stand the diced onion in icy water.

Heat the oil in a wok or heavy frying pan. Add the garlic, chilli paste and julienned lemon rind and stir-fry for 1 minute. Add the mussels, water and lemon juice. Cover and cook over moderate heat, shaking the wok from time to time until the mussels open, about 5-8 minutes. (Discard any mussels that do not open.)

Place the mussels in 4 bowls and top with the juices, drained onion and parsley.

Serve with crusty bread and a salad.

Lamb Stir-fry with Couscous

PREPARATION: 15 minutes • COOKING TIME: 20 minutes • SERVES 4

³/4 cup instant couscous
hot water
600g lean lamb steaks
1 tablespoon rice bran or other
*   vegetable oil*
2 onions, sliced
2–4 teaspoons curry powder or to taste
8 each: pitted dates, dried apricots,
*   chopped*

HINT

- *Couscous is a type of Middle Eastern pasta prepared from semolina. The very fine pellets are quick to prepare.*
- *To make cucumber ribbons, peel thin strips with a potato peeler down the length of the cucumber.*

Place the couscous in a bowl. Add enough very hot water to cover. Stand until the water is absorbed by the couscous.

Cut the lamb into 1cm strips. Heat the oil in a large wok or frying pan and add the onions and curry powder. Add the lamb in batches and stir-fry until cooked. Add the couscous and fruit and cook until hot.

Excellent served with cucumber ribbons, tomatoes, chutney and yoghurt.

DESSERT SUGGESTION

Golden Bananas with Honeyed Yoghurt

1 teaspoon butter or spread
4 small bananas, peeled and halved lengthways
1 tablespoon each: sugar, lemon juice
1 cup plain yoghurt
1–2 tablespoons liquid honey

Heat the butter or spread in a non-stick pan. Add the bananas. Sprinkle with the sugar and lemon juice. Sauté for about 2 minutes until lightly golden at the edges.

Serve with the yoghurt mixed with the honey.

Singapore Beef

PREPARATION: 20 minutes (including 15 minutes marinating time)
COOKING TIME: 8 minutes • SERVES 4

600g sirloin steak
2 teaspoons each: soy sauce, sesame oil,
cornflour
2 tablespoons each: water, canola or
other vegetable oil

Sauce

1 clove garlic, crushed
1 medium onion, sliced
2 teaspoons each: satay sauce, dry
sherry, soy sauce
1 teaspoon each: curry powder, sugar
2 tablespoons water

HINT

* *Crispy noodles are readily available*
  from your supermarket.
* *Prepared satay sauce is available*
  from the Asian section of your
  supermarket. Crunchy peanut
  butter and a dash of chilli could be a
  substitute.

Trim any fat from the meat, then slice the meat into 5mm pieces.

Flatten any thick pieces. Place the meat in a bowl with the combined soy sauce, sesame oil, cornflour and water. Marinate for 15 minutes. Drain.

Heat the oil in a wok or frying pan and sauté the meat quickly in batches until browned. Remove to one side.

To make the sauce, sauté the garlic and onion in the wok until tender. Combine the remaining ingredients and add to the pan. Stir until boiling. Return the meat to the pan to heat through, about 1 minute.

Serve immediately with crispy noodles or rice and a tossed salad.

OVEN
ENTICEMENTS

Chilli Pot

PREPARATION: 30 minutes • COOKING TIME: 2 hours • SERVES 6-8

2 tablespoons canola or other vegetable oil
1kg lean boneless stewing pork or beef or venison, cubed
1 large onion, chopped
1 red or green pepper (capsicum), diced
3 cloves garlic, crushed
1 cup tomato purée
400g can tomatoes in juice
2-4 teaspoons chilli powder or to taste
1 teaspoon sugar
340g can red kidney beans, drained

Preheat the oven to 160°C.

Heat the oil in a saucepan or frying pan suitable for use in the oven. Brown the meat in batches. Remove the meat and set aside once each batch is browned.

Sauté the onion, pepper and garlic until the onion is cooked. Add the tomato purée, tomatoes and juice, chilli powder and sugar.

Bring to the boil, then return the meat to the pan. Cover and place in the oven for $1^{1}/_{2}$ hours or until tender. Add the beans and continue cooking for another 30 minutes.

Great served over baked potatoes that have been split or with corn chips.

HINTS

- *Oven-baked meals mean that – once you have finished the prep – you have lots of time to mingle with the family.*
- *Make full use of your oven. Bake or roast vegetables at the same time as cooking your main course.*
- *Bake or roast fruits for dessert.*
- *This casserole freezes well. If preparing dinner for 4, half may be frozen to use at a later date.*
- *Serve with a simple crisp salad of torn iceberg lettuce, sprinkled with a generous amount of fresh mint leaves, basil and flat-leaf parsley. Drizzle with vinaigrette.*

Quick Thin-crust Pizza

PREPARATION: 20 minutes • COOKING TIME: 20 minutes • SERVES 4

2 cups self-raising flour
$1/4$ teaspoon salt
1 teaspoon dried mixed herbs
2 tablespoons olive oil
$3/4$ cup milk
spray oil

Topping

4-6 tablespoons tomato paste
1 red onion, thinly sliced
4 each: large portabello mushrooms,
   tomatoes, thickly sliced
1 large green pepper (capsicum), seeded
   and thickly sliced
4 rashers rindless bacon, chopped
   (optional)
100g feta cheese, diced
1 teaspoon dried oregano
basil leaves to garnish

Preheat the oven to 190°C. Place an oven tray on a rack to heat. This will help cook the base of the pizza.

To prepare the base, place the flour, salt and mixed herbs in a food processor and mix well. Add the oil and milk and mix until the dough forms a ball. Remove from the food processor and knead lightly on a floured benchtop.

Lightly spray a second oven tray – about 32cm square – with oil. Roll out the dough to fit.

Spread the dough with the tomato paste. Top with rows of onion, mushrooms and tomatoes. Add the green pepper, bacon if using, feta cheese and oregano.

Transfer the pizza to the hot oven tray. Bake for about 20 minutes until the base is browned. Garnish with the basil.

Italian Bean Salad

400g green beans, fresh or frozen
4 ripe tomatoes, quartered
$1/2$ cup black olives, pitted
3 tablespoons coarsely chopped basil leaves
salt and freshly ground pepper to taste
$1/2$ cup balsamic dressing (readily available from your
   supermarket)
2 tablespoons sliced Italian (flat-leaf) parsley to garnish

Trim the beans and slice if necessary. Cook the beans until just tender. Refresh in icy water. Drain well and pat dry.

Combine the beans with the tomatoes, olives, basil and seasonings. Combine with the dressing in a salad bowl. Garnish with the parsley.

Moroccan-style Tagine

PREPARATION: 15 minutes • COOKING TIME: 1¹/₂ hours • SERVES 4-6

600g stewing beef or lamb, cubed, or
    skinned and boned chicken thighs
1 tablespoon olive oil
1 each: large onion, carrot, sliced
1 teaspoon each: ground ginger, turmeric
¹/₂ teaspoon each: ground cinnamon,
    cumin, nutmeg, finely grated orange
    rind
2 tablespoons standard flour
1 cup each: good beef stock, orange juice
¹/₂ cup each: dried apricots, pitted
    prunes, raisins

Preheat the oven to 180°C.

Heat the oil in a large, preferably non-stick, frying pan. Brown the meat in batches. Place in a tagine or casserole.

Add the onion and carrot to the pan with the spices and orange rind and cook for 1-2 minutes, stirring. Add the flour, mixing well.

Pour in the stock and orange juice and bring to the boil. Stir well. Add the apricots, prunes and raisins. Place in the tagine or casserole. Cover and cook in the oven for about 1¹/₂ hours or until the meat is tender.

Serve with rice or couscous.

HINTS

- *Tagines are aromatic stews named after the Middle Eastern container in which they are cooked. Traditionally a tagine is a round casserole-type dish, often made of glazed pottery, with a pointed, conical lid. The tall lid enables the steam to circulate.*
- *To make a herbed couscous, place 1 cup of couscous in a bowl and add enough boiling water to just cover. Stand until the water is absorbed. Stir in 2 tablespoons of butter, salt and pepper to taste and ¹/₂ cup of finely chopped mixed herbs such as parsley, basil, mint and/or marjoram.*

DESSERT SUGGESTION

Melon with Mint
¹/₄ ripe watermelon
1 rock melon
¹/₂ cup fresh mint leaves

Remove the rind and seeds from the melons. Cut the flesh into 2.5cm cubes. Arrange attractively on a platter. Garnish with the mint. Spear the melon pieces with toothpicks.

Rosemary Roasted Lamb

If you like your lamb pink, then it could be roasted at 180-190°C for about 1¹/₄ hours.

PREPARATION: 10 minutes • COOKING TIME: 1¹/₂-2 hours • SERVES 6

1 leg lamb, about 1.5 kg
3 large cloves garlic
3 stalks rosemary
2 tablespoons balsamic vinegar
1 tablespoon olive oil

HINTS

- *Potatoes, kumara and pumpkin can be roasted or baked at the same time. Place in the oven during the last hour of cooking.*
- *Tenting the meat with foil for up to 10 minutes after removing from the oven allows the meat to 'set' and makes it easier to carve.*

Preheat the oven to 170°C.

With the point of a sharp knife, make about 12 small, deep slits in the lamb.

Cut the garlic into slivers. Tear off 12 small sprigs of rosemary. Insert the garlic and rosemary into the slits in the lamb.

Place the meat in a roasting pan. Brush with the combined balsamic vinegar and olive oil.

Roast the lamb for about 1¹/₂-2 hours.

Tent the lamb in foil and leave to stand for about 10 minutes before serving.

Serve the lamb sprinkled with the Parsley Topping accompanied by roast vegetables, gravy and steamed green vegetables.

Parsley Topping

¹/₄ cup finely chopped parsley
grated rind of 1 large lemon
3 cloves garlic
¹/₂ teaspoon salt

Combine the parsley and grated lemon rind.

With the tip of a strong knife, mash the garlic with the salt. Add to the parsley. Sprinkle over the lamb just before serving.

Vegetable & Bacon Frittata

PREPARATION: 10 minutes • COOKING TIME: 50 minutes • SERVES 6

1 large onion, finely sliced
2 tablespoons olive oil
200g rashers rindless middle bacon,
    chopped
500g each: pumpkin, potatoes
$1/4$ cup chopped parsley
freshly ground salt and black pepper
    to taste
6 eggs
$1/4$ cup each: cream, diced red pepper
    (capsicum)

Wild Green Salad

$1/2$ cup olive oil
$1/3$ cup lemon juice
3 cloves garlic, crushed
salt and pepper to taste
1 cos lettuce, torn into small pieces
$1/2$ small telegraph cucumber, sliced
1 cup watercress
4 spring onions, diagonally sliced
$1/4$ cup dill leaves

Whisk together the oil, lemon juice, garlic and seasonings until well mixed.

Combine the greens in a large bowl. Pour the dressing over the salad and toss gently to coat.

In a frying pan sauté the onion in olive oil for 5 minutes or until transparent. Add the bacon and cook for 2 minutes.

Preheat the oven to 180°C.

Peel and seed the pumpkin. Peel the potatoes. Microwave or steam until just tender. Cool and slice.

Lightly oil a 20cm-square baking pan or similar. Line the base with baking paper. Make alternating layers of the potato, pumpkin, onion, bacon and parsley, adding seasoning to each layer.

Beat together the eggs and cream. Pour over the layered mixture and lightly press down. Sprinkle with the diced red pepper. Bake for 35–40 minutes. Cut into squares or oblongs to serve.

HINTS

- Prepare the frittata in advance and reheat in the microwave if preferred.
- Keep sprigs of parsley in the freezer. When you want chopped parsley, clap your hands against the bag of frozen parsley until it crumbles.

Lamb, Pineapple & Chorizo Casserole

PREPARATION: 15 minutes • COOKING TIME: 1^1/$_2$ hours • SERVES 4

4 large lamb shoulder chops
3 tablespoons standard flour
2 tablespoons canola or other vegetable oil
440g can pineapple pieces in juice
2 small chorizo sausages, sliced
1 large onion, sliced
*pinch each: cayenne pepper, ground
   ginger, salt*

DESSERT SUGGESTION

Honeyed-baked Apples

^{1}/$_2$ large orange
1 cup dried apricots, chopped
4 apples
2 tablespoons honey
200g comb honey, optional

Julienne the rind of the half orange. Combine the orange flesh and apricots. Chop finely.

Core the apples with an apple corer. Fill each hollow with the apricot mixture. Arrange the apples in a baking dish just large enough to hold them comfortably.

Dissolve the honey in ^{1}/$_2$ cup of hot water and pour over the apples. Cover with baking paper. Bake for 45-60 minutes until tender, basting occasionally.

To serve, spoon a little comb honey over each baked apple.

Preheat the oven to 180°C.

Remove any excess fat from the meat. Dredge the chops in the flour. Reserve the flour.

Heat the oil in a non-stick frying pan. Lightly brown the chops on both sides. Place in a casserole.

Drain the pineapple, reserving the juice. Lightly brown the pineapple and chorizo in the pan and add to the lamb. Sauté the onions until cooked. Add to the lamb.

Stir in the flour left over from dredging the chops, along with the spices and the reserved pineapple juice. Stir until boiling, then add to the casserole. Cover, place in the oven and cook for 1^1/$_2$ hours.

Great served with baked kumara and green beans.

HINTS
* *To save power, place the Honey-baked Apples in the oven about ^{1}/$_2$ hour after the casserole.*
* *Chorizo is a spicy, coarse-textured sausage. Different manufacturers produce sausages of different strength with 'chilli' heat.*

Sesame-baked Chicken

PREPARATION: 10 minutes • COOKING TIME: 50 minutes • SERVES 4-6

spray oil
1 egg
$^1/_2$ cup milk
$^1/_2$ cup wholemeal flour
1 tablespoon baking powder
$^1/_2$ teaspoon salt
2 tablespoons each: paprika, sesame
   seeds
1 kg chicken portions or drum sticks

HINT

Spray oil is ideal when you want to reduce fat because you only need a very small amount.

Preheat the oven to 180°C. Lightly spray a baking dish with the oil.

Beat the egg and milk together in a small bowl.

Combine the flour, baking powder, salt, paprika and sesame seeds in a plastic bag.

Dip the chicken one piece at a time in the egg mixture, then place in the plastic bag with the flour mixture and shake to coat.

Place the chicken – skin-side up – in the baking dish ensuring the pieces do not touch. Spray with oil. Bake for about 50 minutes or until cooked.

Cheese & Bacon Quiche

PREPARATION: 20 minutes • COOKING TIME: 50 minutes • SERVES 6-8

400g savoury short pastry
6 large eggs
2 1/2 cups cream
salt, pepper, grated nutmeg to taste
200g rindless middle bacon, chopped
1 cup grated Gruyère cheese

HINTS

* *For a vegetarian quiche, omit the bacon.*
* *For variation, add 6 spears of blanched asparagus.*

Roll out the pastry to fit a greased 30cm flan or quiche dish. Trim off any excess pastry. Chill.

Preheat the oven to 190°C. Place an oven tray on a rack to heat. The hot tray helps the base to cook.

Beat together the eggs, cream and seasonings. Sprinkle the bacon over the pastry base. Pour the cream mixture on top. Sprinkle with the cheese.

Bake for 50 minutes or until set and golden.

Quick 'n Easy Chicken Roast with Veggies

A pre-marinated chicken – such as a honey and soy or lime and chilli marinated chicken – could be used for this recipe.

PREPARATION: 15 minutes • COOKING TIME: 1 hour • SERVES 4-5

1.2kg chicken
spray oil
3-4 each: medium potatoes, red onions, carrots, courgettes
4 cloves garlic, sliced
1 large stem rosemary
freshly ground black pepper to taste

DESSERT SUGGESTION

Roasted Peaches & Tamarillos

50g butter, melted
4 red tamarillos, peeled and halved lengthways
4 peaches, halved and stoned
$^1/_4$ cup brown sugar

Preheat the oven to 180°C.

Lightly grease a baking dish. Add the fruit, cut-side up. Drizzle generously with butter and sprinkle with the sugar. Bake until soft.

Serve immediately with whipped cream or ice cream.

Preheat the oven to 180°C.

Insert a large, heavy, sharp knife into the cavity of the chicken and cut down one side of the backbone. Using your hands, flatten the chicken and cut down the other side of the backbone. Remove the backbone and discard.

Spray a roasting pan with oil. Cut the vegetables into thick slices. Place on the base of the roasting pan to make a bed for the chicken. Reserve half the sliced onions for the top. Place the chicken skin-side up on the veggies. Make a couple of slashes in each thigh to ensure the chicken cooks evenly. Sprinkle the remaining onion slices and the garlic and rosemary leaves over the top.

Roast for about 1 hour or until cooked.

Topside Roasted in Spices

PREPARATION: 10 minutes (plus 2-3 hours marinating time)
COOKING TIME: 1¹/₂ hours • SERVES 6-8

Yoghurt Marinade
1 small onion, chopped
1 cup plain yoghurt
4 cloves garlic, chopped
*1 tablespoon each: finely chopped root
    ginger, mustard seeds*
*1 teaspoon each: freshly ground black
    pepper, ground cumin*
¹/₄ teaspoon cayenne pepper

1.5 kg piece beef topside (or bolar)

HINT
*Crisp sliced shallots in icy water. This
helps remove any pungent flavours from
shallots − and onions.*

Combine all the ingredients for the marinade in a blender. Process until smooth. Pour into a plastic bag. Add the beef and move it around in the bag to coat evenly. Marinate for 2-3 hours or overnight in the refrigerator.

Preheat the oven to 160°C.

Place the meat in an oiled roasting pan. Cover loosely with an oven bag. Roast for 30 minutes per 500g meat, basting 2-3 times with the marinade.

The pan juices may be thickened with 2 tablespoons of flour mixed to a paste with a little water. First bring the juices to the boil on the hob, add the paste and stir until thickened. Spoon over the meat.

Excellent served with baked pumpkin or kumara plus a salad of crisp, sliced shallots and oranges.

Roasted Vegetable Lasagne

PREPARATION: 30 minutes • COOKING TIME: 1 hour • SERVES 6

350g fresh lasagne
300g each: kumara, pumpkin (with skin and seeds)
3 tablespoons olive oil
1 teaspoon each: ground cumin, coriander, dried oregano leaves
2 cloves garlic, crushed
250g each: mushrooms, sliced; frozen spinach, thawed
550g jar good pasta sauce
250g ricotta or cottage cheese, beaten
1/2 cup each: grated tasty cheddar, Parmesan cheese

HINT

This dish may be prepared ahead and reheated in the microwave.

Preheat the oven to 180°C.

Lightly oil a 30cm x 22cm baking dish. Cut the lasagne into sheets the same dimensions as the baking dish. If the lasagne is very thick, you may prefer to pre-cook it in boiling water.

Peel the kumara. Peel and seed the pumpkin. Slice the vegetables into 5mm wedges. Place in a roasting pan and toss with 2 tablespoons of olive oil. Sprinkle with the spices and oregano. Roast for 10-15 minutes until just cooked.

Heat the remaining oil and sauté the garlic and mushrooms for 3-4 minutes.

Spoon a little pasta sauce on the base of the prepared baking dish. Make alternating layers of drained lasagne, pumpkin and kumara mix, lasagne, spinach, mushrooms, more lasagne, ricotta or cottage cheese and the remaining pasta sauce.

Cover with foil. Bake at 180°C for 25 minutes. Remove the foil and sprinkle with the grated cheeses. Bake for a further 15 minutes.

Tortellini Bake

PREPARATION: 15 minutes • COOKING TIME: 30 minutes • SERVES 4

*250g asparagus, green beans or broccoli
    florets*
300g fresh chicken tortellini or similar
*2 cups of your favourite pasta sauce or
    white sauce*
1 cup garlic croûtons
200g mozzarella cheese, sliced
$^1/_4$ cup chopped parsley

Slice the asparagus or beans. Blanch the green vegetables in a large saucepan of boiling water until crisp-tender, about 1-2 minutes. Lift out with a slotted spoon and refresh in cold water. Pat dry.

Add the tortellini to the saucepan and cook according to the instructions on the pack. Drain well.

Meanwhile, preheat the oven to 190°C.

Combine the tortellini with the green veggies and sauce and place in a baking dish. Sprinkle with the croutons and dot with the cheese.

Bake for 15-20 minutes. Sprinkle with parsley before serving.

HINT
Make the croûtons by dicing a loaf of garlic bread and toasting in the oven for 5 minutes at 190°C.

Apple & Avocado Salad
1 large avocado
2 tablespoons lemon juice
1-2 crisp apples
2 tablespoons chopped fresh chives

Cider Dressing
2 tablespoons cider vinegar
1 teaspoon each: prepared mustard, sugar
3 tablespoons avocado oil or olive oil

Peel and slice the avocado. Sprinkle with a little lemon juice to prevent discolouration. Quarter, core and slice the apples. Arrange the apples and avocado in a bowl. Sprinkle with lemon juice and chives.

Whisk together the vinegar, mustard and sugar, then slowly add the oil. Drizzle over the salad and serve immediately.

MICROWAVE
MAGIC

Miso Fish

The miso paste in this recipe could be replaced by sweet Thai chilli sauce if preferred. Omit the sugar if taking this option.

600g skinned and boned thick white fish fillets
3 tablespoons miso (soy bean) paste
1^1/2 tablespoons sugar
1 tablespoon rice wine vinegar or cider vinegar

Place the fish in a wide, shallow microwave-proof dish.

Combine the remaining ingredients and brush over the fish. Cover and cook on high (100%) power for about 4-5 minutes.

Excellent served with rice or noodles and steamed or microwaved green vegetables.

HINTS

- *All recipes are microwaved on high (100%) power unless otherwise stated.*
- *Miso, a fermented soybean paste, is a basic flavouring in Japanese cooking. The lighter-coloured versions are used in more delicate dishes, the darker coloured paste features in heavier dishes. Miso is used in sauces, soups, marinades, dips, main dishes, salad dressings and as a table condiment. It is easily digested and extremely nutritious, containing rich amounts of B vitamins and protein.*
- *Check the wattage of your microwave. The higher the wattage the quicker it will cook food. Recipes in this book were developed for a 1000-watt oven.*
- *It is best to undercook — you can always add a few extra seconds or minutes of cooking at the push of a button. However, if microwave food is overcooked it is as bad as when it is overcooked by conventional means.*
- *Always stand food for about one-third of its cooking time before serving.*
- *The more food to be microwaved, the longer it will take. For example, 1 potato may take 2 minutes to cook, 2 potatoes will take about 4 minutes.*
- *Chilled foods take longer to cook than room-temperature foods.*

Chicken Laksa

PREPARATION: 15 minutes • COOKING TIME: 9 minutes • SERVES 4

300g skinned and boned chicken
    breast, cubed
2 tablespoons lemon juice
200g mung bean sprouts
$1/2$ small telegraph cucumber
160g easy-cook, 2-minute, dried
    egg noodles
1 tablespoon canola or other
    vegetable oil
60g (3 tablespoons) packet laksa
    spice paste
$1^1/2$ cups each: coconut milk,
    vegetable stock

Garnish
4 tablespoons chopped coriander
    or mint
2 spring onions, finely sliced

Place the chicken in a bowl and lightly mix with the lemon juice.

Remove any brown ends from the bean sprouts. Cut the cucumber into matchstick-sized pieces. Set aside.

Cook the noodles according to the instructions on the pack.

Place the oil in a microwave-proof bowl and stir in the spice paste. Microwave on high (100%) power for 30 seconds. Transfer the spice paste to a saucepan along with the coconut milk and vegetable stock and bring to the boil. Simmer for 4 minutes. Add the chicken and heat through for 3-4 minutes until cooked.

Drain the noodles. Place in 4 deep serving bowls and top with the bean sprouts, cucumber, soup and chicken. Garnish with coriander or mint and the spring onions.

DESSERT SUGGESTION

Feijoa & Berry Crumble
6 feijoas
1 cup fresh or frozen cranberries or
    raspberries
3 tablespoons sugar
finely grated rind and juice of 1 lemon
1 tablespoon custard powder

Crumble Topping
1 cup rolled oats
$1/4$ cup packed brown sugar
$1/2$ teaspoon ground cinnamon
50g chilled butter, chopped

Peel and thickly slice the feijoas into a bowl. Add the cranberries or raspberries, sugar, lemon rind and juice. Mix well. Stand for 30 minutes for the juices to develop. Stir in the custard powder. Divide the mixture evenly between 4 individual ramekins.

Combine the ingredients for the crumble, rubbing the butter in with your fingertips. Spoon over the fruit.

Microwave for 4-5 minutes or until the fruit is cooked and bubbling. The top may be browned under the oven grill, if preferred.

Mediterranean-style Fish

PREPARATION: 10 minutes • COOKING TIME: 10 minutes • SERVES 4

1 tablespoon olive oil
$^1/_2$ each: red, green pepper (capsicum),
    seeded and chopped
2 spring onions, chopped
2 large tomatoes, seeded and chopped
2 stalks celery, diced
2 cloves garlic, crushed
freshly ground black pepper to taste
700g skinned and boned white
    fish fillets
2 teaspoons capers, rinsed and dried

Combine all the ingredients – except the fish and capers – in a bowl. Cover and cook on high (100%) power for 3 minutes. Cool.

Ensure the pieces of fish are evenly sized. Place the fish in a large, shallow microwave-proof dish. Overlap any thin pieces of fish. Spoon the vegetable mixture over the top. Cover.

Microwave for 5-7 minutes. Serve garnished with the capers.

Great served with crusty bread and a salad.

DESSERT SUGGESTION

Peach Surprise
Nectarines could replace the peaches.

4 peaches
juice of 1 orange
8 tablespoons fruit mince
3-4 tablespoons sliced almonds

Halve and stone the peaches.

Place in a microwave-proof dish, cut-side up. Brush with the orange juice. Heat in the microwave on high (100%) power for 1-2 minutes.

Fill the centres with the fruit mince and heat for a further 3-4 minutes. Sprinkle with the almonds before serving. Excellent served 'as is' or with custard, cream or ice cream.

Mexican Meatloaf

PREPARATION: 15 minutes
COOKING TIME: 24 minutes (including standing time) • SERVES 8

4 slices sandwich-sliced white bread,
   crusts removed
1 small onion, quartered
4 cloves garlic
1 red pepper (capsicum), seeded and
   chopped
2-3 teaspoons chilli paste or chopped
   fresh chilli
1kg lean minced beef
1 large egg

Sauce
1 1/2 cups Mexican-style salsa
2 tablespoons lemon juice
chilli to taste

HINT
This recipe makes enough to serve
2 meals for 4 people. The loaf can be
served hot or cold.

Place the bread in a food processor and mix until crumbed. Add the onion, garlic and red pepper until finely chopped.

Add the other ingredients, mixing very well.

Pat the mixture firmly into a microwave-proof loaf pan or ring mould.

Place on a rack in the microwave. Cover with a paper towel. Cook on half (50%) power for 6 minutes. Stand for 6 minutes, then continue cooking on half power for another 6 minutes. Stand for 6 minutes. Drain off the liquid before slicing thinly to serve.

Combine the ingredients for the sauce and heat through on high (100%) power. Serve over the sliced meat loaf.

Excellent topped with chopped fresh coriander and accompanied by slices of avocado and corn chips.

The Kids' Baked Stuffed Potatoes

PREPARATION: 10 minutes • COOKING TIME: 10 minutes • SERVES 4

4 medium potatoes, washed
25g butter
2 tablespoons each: milk, chopped
    parsley
1 cup grated cheddar cheese
$^1/_2$ cup chopped ham
salt and pepper to taste

Topping
2 tablespoons chopped parsley
$^1/_2$ cup grated cheddar cheese

HINTS
- *Kids love to prepare these spuds. Let them add some of their own fillings, eg diced frankfurters, chopped peppers (capsicums), or left-over Bolognese sauce.*
- *Great served with a crisp green salad or steamed asparagus.*

Using the point of a skewer, prick the potatoes in several places. Arrange the potatoes on a paper towel on a microwave turntable.

Microwave on high (100%) power for about 4 minutes. Turn the potatoes over and continue cooking until soft, about 2 minutes. Cool for a few minutes.

Cut the potatoes in half lengthways. Using a teaspoon, scoop out the potato flesh and place in a bowl.

Mash the potato flesh with the butter and milk. Add the parsley, cheese, ham and seasonings.

Spoon the mixture back into the potatoes. Top with the extra parsley and cheese.

Microwave for 3-4 minutes until hot, and serve.

Hot Potato Salad

PREPARATION: 5 minutes • COOKING TIME: 15 minutes • SERVES 4

4 medium potatoes
3 rashers rindless bacon, diced
1 small onion, diced
$1^1/_2$ tablespoons standard flour
1 tablespoon sugar
salt and pepper to taste
1 teaspoon mustard powder
$^1/_2$ cup water
$^1/_4$ cup white vinegar
4 frankfurters

HINTS

- *To find whether a dish is suitable for microwave cooking, place the empty container in the microwave with a cup of cold water alongside. Microwave for 1 minute. If the water is warm and the dish cold, then the container is suitable for microwave cooking. If the container is hot and the water cold, then the dish has absorbed the microwaves and is not suitable. This is sometimes the case with home-made pottery.*
- *Most dishes these days carry microwave and dishwasher-safe markings. Do not use china with metallic decorations or fine bone china as they could cause arcing in the microwave.*
- *Plastic microwave ware should retain its rigidity during cooking to ensure hot food is not spilt when being removed from the oven. Plastic ware should carry a microwave-safe marking.*

Wash and halve the potatoes. Place on a microwave-proof plate and cover loosely with waxed paper. Microwave on high (100%) power for 5–6 minutes or until soft.

Place the bacon and onion in a large microwave-proof bowl. Microwave for 3 minutes. Stir in the flour, sugar, seasonings, water and vinegar. Microwave for 1 minute. Stir well, then continue cooking for 2 minutes.

Cut the potatoes into cubes.

Cut each frankfurter into 6 pieces. Place in a shallow microwave-proof baking dish. Cover loosely and microwave on high (100%) power for 1 minute. Combine the potatoes with the franks. Pour the sauce over the top. Toss to coat evenly. Reheat for 2 minutes, if necessary.

Great served sprinkled with ground paprika and chopped fresh parsley and accompanied by a green salad.

Vegetable Chilli

PREPARATION: 15 minutes • COOKING TIME: 20 minutes • SERVES 4

1 onion, diced
2 cloves garlic, crushed
1 large carrot, diced
250g mushrooms, diced
$^1/_4$ cup vegetable stock
1 courgette, diced
400g can chilli beans, drained
$^1/_2$ teaspoon chilli paste (optional)

Microwave Rice

1 cup long grain rice, washed
2 cups water
pinch of salt

Place the ingredients in a deep 3-litre microwave-proof casserole or bowl. Cook for 10 minutes on high (100%) power, stirring twice during cooking. Cook until the rice has absorbed most of the water. Stir, cover and stand for 5 minutes to absorb the remaining water. Fluff with a fork before serving.

HINT

To make star-shaped rice, pack the rice into an oblong dish. Upturn onto a chopping board. Use a biscuit cutter to make the shapes.

Place the onion, garlic, carrot, mushrooms and stock in a large microwave-proof casserole. Cover and microwave on high (100%) power for 5 minutes. Stir well, add the courgette, and continue cooking for 5 minutes.

Add the beans and chilli paste, if using. Mix well, cover, and microwave for 10 minutes, stirring occasionally.

Excellent served with rice.

Microwave Enchiladas

PREPARATION: 10 minutes • COOKING TIME: 15 minutes • SERVES 4-6

500g lean minced beef
400g can tomato purée
$^1/_2$ cup water
2 cups grated tasty cheddar cheese
$^1/_2$ cup sliced green olives
1-2 teaspoons chilli paste
6 flour tortillas

Place the minced beef in a large microwave-proof bowl and stir with a fork. Cook on high (100%) power for 1 minute. Stir well and continue cooking for 3 minutes. Stir in 1 cup of purée, the water, 1 cup of cheese and the olives. Microwave for 2 minutes.

Combine the remaining tomato purée with the chilli paste. Pour in enough sauce to cover the base of a 28cm x 21cm microwave-proof baking dish.

Place 2 large spoonfuls of the meat onto each tortilla and roll up. Place in the baking dish and spoon the remaining sauce over the tortillas, ensuring they are well coated. Sprinkle with the remaining cheese. Cover and microwave for 4-5 minutes until very hot. Brown under the oven grill if preferred.

HINTS

- *Choose microwave-safe plastic film for short periods of cooking only. Very hot food touching the film causes the film to melt.*
- *Paper towels absorb excess moisture from breads, cakes and pies during reheating. Stand foods on paper towels to heat.*
- *Paper plates can be used for short periods of cooking or reheating or for covering foods during cooking.*

DESSERT SUGGESTION

Berry Fool

$1^1/_2$ cups fresh or frozen blackcurrants or blueberries
3 tablespoons water
$^1/_2$ cup sugar
1 cup cream, whipped

Place the berries in a large microwave-proof bowl. Add the water and sugar. Stir well. Cover and microwave on high (100%) power for 4-5 minutes until soft.

Purée in a blender. Sieve, if preferred. Cool. Fold in the whipped cream. Chill.

Chicken & Spinach Cannelloni

PREPARATION: 30 minutes • COOKING TIME: 20 minutes • SERVES 6

Filling

1 tablespoon olive oil

1 small onion, chopped

4 cloves garlic, crushed

350g (1 bag) spinach, washed and
    chopped

600g minced chicken

3 tablespoons each: finely grated
    Parmesan cheese, cream

1 large egg, lightly beaten

2 teaspoons dried oregano

salt and pepper to taste

12 tubes cannelloni

Topping

2 cups (500g) ricotta cheese or
    lite sour cream

1 1/2 cups good quality tomato pasta
    sauce or tomato purée

1/4 cup finely grated Parmesan cheese

HINT

This recipe can be prepared ahead to the final cooking stage, then refrigerated. If chilled, the dish may need a little extra cooking time. A great dish for family and friends.

Place half the oil in a large microwave-proof bowl and add the onion and garlic. Cover and cook on high (100%) power for 2 minutes. Add the spinach and cook for 2 minutes. Drain well and squeeze dry.

Place the remaining oil in the clean bowl. Using a large fork, stir in the minced chicken. Microwave for 6 minutes on medium (50%) power, stirring well after each 2 minutes of cooking. Combine with the spinach mixture. Add the Parmesan, cream, egg and seasonings.

Meanwhile, cook the cannelloni in a large saucepan of boiling water on the stovetop until just tender. Drain well, cool and pat dry. Spoon the chicken mixture into the tubes.

Whisk the ricotta or sour cream. Spoon a thin layer of the tomato pasta sauce into the base of a 30cm x 20cm microwave-proof oblong dish. Place the cannelloni on top in a single layer. Cover with the ricotta or sour cream, then the remaining purée.

Sprinkle with the Parmesan cheese just before cooking. Cover and microwave on half (50%) power for about 10 minutes or until bubbling. Place under a preheated oven grill to brown if preferred.

Tikka Masala Lamb with Pappadums

PREPARATION: 15 minutes • COOKING TIME: 50 minutes • SERVES 4

500g lamb leg steaks
1 tablespoon rice bran oil or canola oil
1 bay leaf
1 onion, sliced
2-3 tablespoons Tikka Masala curry paste or similar
1 tablespoon flour
1 cup sour cream
freshly ground black pepper to taste
8 pappadums

HINT

As with conventional cooking, tougher cuts of meat require longer, slower cooking. Stews and the less expensive meat cuts should be cooked on medium (50%) or low (30%) power. A casserole using 500g of stewing meat can take up to 1 hour to cook on low power depending on the number of other ingredients included. After removing from the oven, stand the food (covered) for about one-third of the cooking time before serving.

Trim the leg steaks of any excess fat and cut into cubes. Brown the lamb on both sides in the oil in a conventional frying pan. Place the meat in a single layer in a shallow microwave-proof casserole. Add the bay leaf.

Brown the onion in the pan. Remove from the heat. Stir in the curry paste, flour and sour cream, then pour over the lamb. Sprinkle with pepper.

Cover and cook on low (30%) power for 40-45 minutes, until tender. Stir halfway through. Stand, covered, for 10 minutes before serving.

While the lamb is standing, cook the pappadums in batches. Place them 4 at a time on a paper towel in the microwave and cook on high (100%) power for 2-3 minutes until the pappadums are puffed and crisp. Repeat.

Serve the lamb with steamed rice, chutneys, diced cucumber, diced kiwifruit and yoghurt.

Hot Gado Gado

PREPARATION: 10 minutes • COOKING TIME: 12 minutes • SERVES 4

Peanut Sauce

1 tablespoon vegetable oil
1 onion, diced
$^1/_2$ teaspoon diced chilli
$^1/_2$ cup crunchy peanut butter
1 cup water
2 teaspoons soy sauce
1 tablespoon lemon juice

Salad

3 medium potatoes
1 large carrot
150g frozen green beans
1 tablespoon water
$1^1/_2$ cups finely shredded cabbage
1 onion, thinly sliced

HINT

To microwave green veggies, first cut them into similar-sized pieces. Place in a suitable microwave-proof serving dish. Add a sprinkle of water. Cover with microwave film or a lid and microwave until just cooked.

To make the sauce, place the oil and onion in a microwave-proof bowl and cook on high (100%) power for 1 minute. Add the remaining ingredients for the sauce. Stir well and microwave for 2 minutes.

Pierce each potato with a fork. Place the unpeeled potatoes on paper towels in the microwave. Cover with a paper towel and microwave on high (100%) power for about 5 minutes or until cooked.

Peel and cut the carrot into thin batons. Place in a microwave-proof shallow dish with the beans. Sprinkle with the water. Cover and microwave on high (100%) power for about 3 minutes, until hot and just cooked.

Slice the potatoes onto a serving plate. Layer the other cooked vegetables on top. Reheat if necessary. Top with the shredded cabbage and garnish with the onion. Pour the hot peanut sauce on top just before serving.

Excellent topped with diced spring onions and served with rice and sliced tomatoes.

Savoury Peppers with Smoked Chicken

PREPARATION: 5 minutes • COOKING TIME: 4-6 minutes • SERVES 4

4 red peppers (capsicums)
350g skinned and boned smoked
  chicken
$^3/_4$ cup cooked rice
2 each: small onions, celery stalks, diced
4 tablespoons mayonnaise
freshly ground black pepper to taste
2 teaspoons prepared mustard
$^1/_3$ cup chopped parsley

Cut the peppers in half lengthways and remove the seeds and ribs. Place on a dish suitable for microwave cooking. Cover with microwave-safe plastic film, piercing the top to prevent it from bursting. Cook on high (100%) power for 1-2 minutes.

Mince the chicken in a food processor.

Combine the chicken with the rice, onion, celery, mayonnaise, black pepper and mustard and half the parsley. Pack the mixture into the peppers.

Microwave on high for 2-4 minutes. Sprinkle with the remaining parsley before serving.

SLOW
COOKER
COMFORTS

Devilled Lamb Shanks

PREPARATION: 15 minutes • COOKING TIME: 6-8 hours • SERVES 4

1 onion, chopped
2 cloves garlic, chopped
1 tablespoon vegetable oil
4 medium lamb shanks
$^1/_2$ cup red wine
400g can condensed tomato soup
1 tablespoon each: Worcestershire sauce,
    wine vinegar, honey

Sauté the onion and garlic in oil in a non-stick frying pan until softened. Place in a slow cooker.

Sauté the lamb shanks in the pan until lightly browned. Place on top of the onion mixture in the slow cooker.

Add the wine to the pan and bring to the boil. Stir to dislodge any pieces of meat and onion that may have stuck to the base. Add the tomato soup, Worcestershire sauce, vinegar and honey. Mix well. Pour over the shanks.

Cover and cook on low for 6-8 hours.

Great served with soft polenta (see page 121).

HINTS
* To obtain the best flavour, lightly brown the meat and veggies before placing them in the slow cooker. However, if time is limited, this step can be eliminated. It is important though, to pre-cook onion either by sautéeing in a frying pan or in the microwave, as raw onion can sometimes dominate the flavours.
* A slow cooker normally has a removable ceramic insert from which you can serve the meal at the table. Or, when cooled, it can be stored in the refrigerator and reheated in the microwave.
* If you want to convert a favourite recipe that normally takes 1 hour to cook conventionally at 160°C, allow 6-8 hours in a slow cooker set on low.

Mediterranean Pot Roast

Two diced parsnips or carrots could be added to this pot roast.

PREPARATION: 15 minutes • COOKING TIME: 8 hours • SERVES 6

1.3kg piece beef bolar or topside
freshly ground black pepper to taste
4–5 streaky bacon rashers
2 tablespoons olive oil
1 large leek or onion, thickly sliced
4 sprigs rosemary
10 cloves garlic, whole
$^1/_4$ cup each: good beef stock or jus,
*   balsamic vinegar*
400g can Italian-style tomatoes

HINT

'Jus' is the French word for the 'juice'
which normally refers to the natural juices
obtained from cooked meat. However, it
can also refer to both fruit and vegetable
juices, eg 'jus de citron' is orange juice.

Season the beef with black pepper. Wrap the bacon around the meat. Heat the oil in a large pan. Sauté the beef until lightly coloured. Set aside.

Sauté the leek or onion until softened. Place in the slow cooker. Place 2 sprigs of rosemary on top then add the meat. Top with the remaining rosemary, the peeled garlic, stock, balsamic vinegar and tomatoes in their juice.

Cover and cook on low for 8 hours. Remove the meat to a carving platter. The sauce can be thickened with a little flour, if preferred.

Soft Polenta with Cheese

2 cups milk
$^1/_2$ cup instant polenta
3 tablespoons butter
$^1/_4$ cup each: chopped parsley; crumbled mild blue cheese
*   or grated tasty cheddar cheese*
salt and pepper to taste

To prepare the polenta, bring the milk to boiling point in a saucepan or a bowl in the microwave. Slowly pour in the polenta, stirring continuously. Simmer, stirring for about 5 minutes, until thick.

Add the butter, parsley, cheese and seasonings. Mix well.

Sweet 'n Sour Ribs

PREPARATION: 10 minutes
COOKING TIME: 8 hours or 4-5 hours, depending on method • SERVES 4

1.2kg pork ribs, uncut
3-4 tablespoons flour
3 tablespoons each: maple syrup, soy
   sauce, barbecue sauce, balsamic
   vinegar
1 teaspoon mustard
400g can pineapple pieces in juice

Savoury Melon Salad

1 cup peeled, seeded and diced rock melon
1 large avocado, peeled, stoned and thickly
   sliced
8 cherry tomatoes, halved
2 tablespoons each: chopped chives, basil
$^{1}/_{4}$ cup lemon juice
2 tablespoons avocado or olive oil
salt and freshly ground pepper to taste

Combine the rock melon, avocado,
tomatoes, herbs and 1 tablespoon of the
lemon juice in a bowl. Whisk the remaining
ingredients and drizzle over the salad just
before serving.

If necessary, cut the ribs into smaller slabs so they will
fit neatly into the slow cooker. Cut close to one side
of the bone so there is lots of meat on the other side.
Place the ribs in a plastic bag with the flour and shake
to coat.

Combine the next 5 ingredients. Brush over the ribs.
Place in the slow cooker, standing the ribs up to fit
neatly. Add the pineapple pieces and juice. Cover and
cook on low for 8 hours or on high for 4-5 hours.

Excellent served with a combined mash of sautéed
onion, steamed pumpkin and broccoli.

Easy Vietnamese Chicken

PREPARATION: 10 minutes • COOKING TIME: 8 hours • SERVES 6

1.5kg whole chicken
1/2 cup chicken stock
2 tablespoons each: soy sauce,
    fish sauce, lime or lemon juice
2 teaspoons brown sugar
1 teaspoon sesame oil
3 kaffir lime leaves or young lemon
    leaves
1 bunch each: coriander, basil leaves
1-2 each: whole chillies, garlic cloves

Pat the chicken dry, inside and out, with a paper towel. Tie or truss to retain a neat shape. Place in the slow cooker.

Combine the chicken stock, soy sauce, fish sauce, lime juice, brown sugar and sesame oil. Pour over the chicken. Top with the lime leaves, herbs, chillies and peeled garlic.

Cover and cook the chicken on low for 8 hours.

Excellent served with steamed rice and a salad of pawpaw or peaches tossed in lemon juice and chopped coriander leaves and stalks.

Pork Steaks with Orange-Mustard Sauce

PREPARATION: 5 minutes
COOKING TIME: 6-7 hours or 3-3$^{1}/_{2}$ hours, depending on method • SERVES 4-6

4-6 pork steaks (about 700g), cut
   2.5cm thick
salt and pepper to taste
2 teaspoons chopped thyme leaves
1 cup orange marmalade
4 tablespoons Dijon-style mustard
$^{1}/_{4}$ cup water

HINTS

- Very little moisture is lost from slow cookers, so if you're converting a favourite recipe, reduce the amount of liquid by one-third to one-half. Little or no stirring is required when cooking on low. However, if using the high temperature on the control, then occasional stirring may be necessary to distribute the heat evenly.
- As a rule, most foods – except dried beans – can be cooked on high or low settings.
- When you take off the lid for a peek, the cooker loses heat. Therefore, the food will take longer to cook.
- Reheating leftovers in a slow cooker is not recommended.

Trim the steaks of any fat. Sprinkle both sides with salt, pepper and the chopped thyme. Press into the meat. Place in a lightly oiled slow cooker.

In a bowl combine the orange marmalade, mustard and water. Pour over the steaks. Cover and cook on low for 6-7 hours or on high for 3-3$^{1}/_{2}$ hours.

Transfer the steaks to a serving platter. Strain the cooking liquid. Spoon over the steaks.

Excellent served with a potato or kumara mash and broccoli florets that have been threaded onto skewers and steamed until just tender.

Carbonnade

PREPARATION: 15 minutes • COOKING TIME: 6-8 hours • SERVES 4

1 onion, chopped
2 each: celery stalks, carrots, diced
1 green pepper (capsicum),
    seeded and diced
1-2 tablespoons olive oil
750g stewing beef, cubed
3 tablespoons standard flour
salt and pepper to taste
2 tablespoons mustard
1^1/2 cups lager

Sauté the onion, celery, carrots and green pepper in a non-stick frying pan in a tablespoon of the oil, until lightly coloured. Place in the slow cooker.

Toss the beef in the flour seasoned with salt and pepper. Lightly brown in the remaining oil. Add to the vegetables.

Combine the mustard and beer and pour over the meat. Stir well. Cover and cook on low for 6-8 hours.

Great served with Crostini Parmesan.

Crostini Parmesan
1 small French stick
4-5 tablespoons Dijon-style mustard
^{3}/4 cup finely grated Parmesan cheese

Preheat the grill. Slice the bread into 1cm-thick rounds. Lightly toast both sides under the grill.

Spread one side with a little mustard and sprinkle with the cheese. Place back under the grill until the cheese melts a little.

HINTS
- Ask your children to peel the carrots for the carbonade and grate the cheese for the crostini.
- Any alcohol used in cooking will evaporate as it is heated. Beer in recipes can often be replaced by a good stock; and wine with a tangy clear apple juice.

Roast Pork with Apricots

PREPARATION: 10 minutes • COOKING TIME: 8 hours • SERVES 6

spray oil
1 large onion, chopped
1.5kg piece boneless pork
$^3/_4$ cup chicken stock
$^1/_2$ cup chopped dried apricots
410g can apricot halves, drained
1 tablespoon each: balsamic vinegar,
*   lemon juice, brown sugar*

Spray a non-stick frying pan with the oil. Lightly sauté the onion and place in the slow cooker. Brown the pork lightly all over. Place on top of the onion in the slow cooker.

Combine the remaining ingredients and pour over the pork. Cover and cook for 8 hours on low.

Serve with couscous or crusty bread and a crisp green salad.

Salad Greens with Lime Dressing

4-5 cups loosely packed salad greens
$^1/_4$ cup lime juice
2 cloves garlic, crushed
2 tablespoons chopped coriander leaves
freshly ground black pepper to taste
2 teaspoons each: fish sauce, sugar

Place the salad greens in a bowl. Whisk the remaining ingredients and drizzle over the greens just before serving.

HINT

Spray oil is ideal when you want to reduce fat because you only need a very small amount.

Lamb with Asian Spices

PREPARATION: 10 minutes • COOKING TIME: 8 hours • SERVES 6

1.6kg leg lamb
1 teaspoon five-spice powder
2 tablespoons each: standard flour,
    canola or other vegetable oil,
    red wine vinegar, oyster sauce,
    soy sauce
1 tablespoon each: sambal oeleck,
    hoisin sauce
4 cloves garlic, crushed
2 cups good beef stock
2 each: cinnamon sticks, star anise

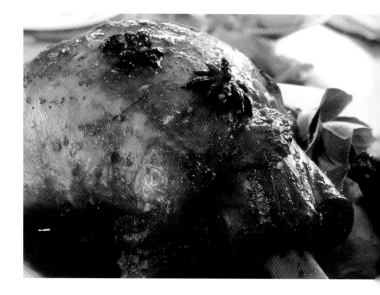

Trim the lamb of any excess fat. Combine the five-spice powder with the flour. Rub onto the lamb. Place in a slow cooker.

Combine all the other ingredients in a saucepan and bring to the boil. Pour over the lamb. Cover and cook on low for 8 hours.

Remove the lamb to a warm platter and leave to rest. Strain the sauce into a small saucepan. Bring to the boil and reduce until slightly thickened. Alternatively, thicken with 2 tablespoons of cornflour mixed to a paste with $1/4$ cup of water. Stir over low heat until thick.

Serve with the lamb along with mashed potatoes flavoured with crushed garlic or wasabi.

Red Lentil Hotpot

PREPARATION: 15 minutes • COOKING TIME: 5-6 hours • SERVES 6

1 tablespoon canola or other
    vegetable oil
2 each: onions, carrots, finely diced
1-2 tablespoons curry powder
1$^{1}/_{2}$ cups each: red lentils, peeled and
    diced kumara
3 cups vegetable stock
3 cloves garlic, crushed
1 green pepper (capsicum), diced
400g can tomatoes in juice, chopped

Garnish
yoghurt to taste
coriander leaves

Heat the oil in a large, non-stick frying pan. Add the onions and carrots and cook until the onions are soft. Stir in the curry powder, then place the mixture in a slow cooker.

Wash the lentils well. Add to the slow cooker.

Add all the remaining ingredients to the lentils. Cover and cook on low for 5-6 hours. Serve in bowls garnished with the yoghurt and coriander leaves. A crisp salad and crusty bread make delicious accompaniments.

DESSERT SUGGESTION

Quick Brulée
425g can guavas or similar, drained
$^{3}/_{4}$ cup lite sour cream
$^{1}/_{2}$ teaspoon finely grated lemon rind
$^{1}/_{2}$ cup brown sugar

Preheat the grill.

Drain the guavas well and slice. Divide evenly between 4 small heatproof ramekins or soufflé dishes.

Combine the sour cream with the lemon rind and spoon over the fruit. Sprinkle each one evenly with brown sugar.

Cook under the grill until the sugar caramelises. Serve immediately.

Serves 4

Chicken with Herbs

PREPARATION: 20 minutes • COOKING TIME: 8 hours • SERVES 6

1 each: large carrot, onion, diced
3 cloves garlic, crushed
1-2 tablespoons olive oil
6 chicken legs, skinned
large bunch mixed fresh herbs, eg
*   rosemary, thyme, sage, parsley,*
*   bay leaves*
salt and pepper
1^1/$_2$ cups dry white wine or clear
*   unsweetened apple juice*
100g each: button mushrooms,
*   baby carrots, baby onions*

HINTS

- *The baby onions may be steamed or microwaved before adding to the cooker.*
- *When making the dessert, you can use drained, canned pear halves to save time.*

Lightly sauté the carrot, onion and garlic in 1 tablespoon of the olive oil in a non-stick frying pan, until the onion is softened. Place in the slow cooker.

Lightly brown the chicken in the remaining olive oil. Place on top of the vegetables in the slow cooker. Tie the herbs together and add to the bowl.

Season to taste. Add the wine or apple juice, mushrooms, carrots and onions. Cover and cook for 8 hours on low.

DESSERT SUGGESTION

Pears with Walnut Cream

^{3}/4 cup each: walnut pieces, prepared custard
^{1}/2 cup cream
6 poached pears

Lightly toast the walnuts in the microwave or conventional oven (180°C for 10 minutes). Cool then coarsely chop. Combine with the custard.

Whip the cream until soft peaks form. Fold into the walnut mixture. Chill. Serve over the warmed or room-temperature pears.

Saucy Meatballs

PREPARATION: 20 minutes • COOKING TIME: 6 hours • SERVES 6-8

250g mushrooms, sliced

2 red or green peppers (capsicums), sliced

1 cup prepared stuffing mix

750g lean minced beef

1 egg, lightly beaten

$^1/_2$ cup water

3 cups (750ml) good quality pasta sauce

1 tablespoon each: brown sugar, Worcestershire sauce, vinegar

salt and freshly ground black pepper to taste

Place the prepared mushrooms and peppers in the slow cooker.

Combine the stuffing mix, minced beef, egg and water. Form the mixture into golf ball-sized meat balls. Place on top of the vegetables.

Combine the pasta sauce, brown sugar, Worcestershire sauce, vinegar, salt and pepper and pour over the top.

Cover and cook on low for 6 hours.

Excellent served with spaghetti and garnished with grated Parmesan cheese.

HINTS

- Don't leave leftovers sitting in the slow cooker. Remove them, cool and refrigerate or freeze.
- Ensure frozen foods are thawed before you start cooking them in the slow cooker.
- Pasta should be cooked until just tender or 'al dente'. Bring a large saucepan of water to the boil, adding a little salt. Slowly add the pasta to the boiling water – do not allow the water to go off the boil – stir the pasta a little to prevent initial sticking, then cook at a rolling boil.

Fragrant Beef Curry

PREPARATION: 20 minutes • COOKING TIME: 6-8 hours • SERVES 6

1kg stewing beef, cut into 3cm cubes
salt and pepper to taste
3 tablespoons canola or other
vegetable oil
2 large onions, diced
2-3 tablespoons Thai red curry paste
1 each: cinnamon stick, bay leaf
2-3 teaspoons each: crushed garlic,
grated root ginger, lemon juice
1 cup coconut milk
432g can pineapple pieces in juice

Sprinkle the beef with salt and pepper. Heat 2 tablespoons of the oil in a large, heavy saucepan over high heat. Brown the beef in batches, removing each batch from the pan after it has browned. Set aside.

Heat the remaining oil in the same saucepan over medium-high heat. Add the onions and sauté, until tender and golden. Add the curry paste, stir for 30 seconds. Transfer the mixture to the slow cooker.

Add the beef to the slow cooker. Add the remaining spices, garlic and ginger and stir well. Pour in the lemon juice, coconut milk, pineapple pieces and juice. Cover and cook on low for 6-8 hours.

Excellent served with steamed rice.

HINT

If you're in a hurry to prepare this dish, omit browning the beef. Cook the onions quickly in the microwave, stir in the curry paste, then add this mixture to the slow cooker.

DESSERT SUGGESTION

Raspberry Profiteroles

1 cup cream
2 tablespoons icing sugar
1 cup raspberries
1 packet profiteroles
icing sugar for dusting

Whip the cream with the icing sugar. Lightly crush the raspberries and mix through the cream.

Halve the profiteroles and fill with the raspberry cream. Dust with icing sugar before serving.

Weights & Measures

Recipes in this book use standard, level, metric measurements.

In New Zealand, England and the USA 1 tablespoon equals 15ml. In Australia, 1 tablespoon equals 20ml. The variation will not normally greatly affect the result of a recipe apart from some bakes and cakes.

If preferred, use 3 teaspoons rather than 1 Australian tablespoon for measures of raising agents and spices.

GRAMS TO OUNCES

These are converted to the nearest measurable number.

GRAMS		OUNCES
25	=	1
50	=	2
75	=	3
100	=	3.5
125	=	4
150	=	5
175	=	6
200	=	7
225	=	8
250	=	9
275	=	10
300	=	10.5
325	=	11
350	=	12
375	=	13
400	=	14
425	=	15
450	=	16

1kg = 1000g = 2lb 4oz

ABBREVIATIONS

METRIC

g	grams
kg	kilograms
mm	millimetre
cm	centimetre
ml	millilitre
°C	degree Celsius

OVEN SETTING EQUIVALENTS (TO NEAREST 10°C)

	FAHRENHEIT	CELSIUS	GAS REGULO NO
Very cool	225-275	110-140	$^1/_4$-1
Cool	300-325	150-160	2-3
Moderate	350-375	180-190	4-5
Hot	400-450	200-230	6-8
Very hot	475-500	250-260	9-10

CUP & SPOON MEASURES
(TO NEAREST ROUND NUMBER)

	METRIC
	METRIC
$^1/_4$ cup	60ml
$^1/_2$ cup	125ml
1 cup	250ml
2 cups	500ml
4 cups	1000ml
	or 1 litre
1 teaspoon	5ml
1 dessertspoon	10ml
1 tablespoon	15ml
2 teaspoons	1 dessertspoon
3 teaspoons	1 tablespoon
16 tablespoons	1 cup

MEASURES OF LENGTH

CM		APPROX. INCHES
0.5	=	$^1/_4$
1	=	$^1/_2$
2.5	=	1
5	=	2
15	=	6
18	=	7
20	=	8
23	=	9
25	=	10
30	=	12

APPROXIMATE VOLUMES & WEIGHTS OF COMMON FOOD INGREDIENTS

INGREDIENT		VOLUME	WEIGHT
breadcrumbs – dry		1 cup	150g
– fresh		1 cup	60g
butter		1 cup	250g
		1 tablespoon	15g
cheese, grated		1 cup (packed)	100g
flour	– white	1 cup	125g
		2 tablespoons	15g
	– wholemeal	1 cup	125g
currants, sultanas, raisins		1 cup	160-175g
desiccated coconut		1 cup	250ml
mushrooms, sliced		1 cup	75g (4-5 med)
peanuts		1 cup	150g
potatoes, mashed		1 cup	300g (2 med)
pumpkin, mashed		1 cup	500g (with skin & seeds)
rice		1 cup	225g
sugar	– white	1 cup	250g
	– caster	1 cup	250g
	– brown soft-packed	1 cup	150g
	– brown firm-packed	1 cup	200g
	– icing	1 cup	125g
spinach		1 bunch (bag)	350g
walnuts, halves		1 cup	100g
yoghurt		1 cup	250ml

Glossary

Baste: to spoon juices or marinade over foods being roasted, grilled or barbecued to add flavour or to glaze the surface.

Blanch: to place food briefly in boiling water to partly cook, to soften, to remove skins or strong flavours, or to set colours before freezing.

Boil: to cook in water at 100°C.

Bouquet Garni: a bunch of herbs traditionally made up of 2-3 stalks of parsley, a sprig of thyme and a bay leaf tied with string for easy removal.

Cream: to beat with a spoon or electric mixer until soft, smooth and fluffy, as in creaming butter and sugar.

Cube: to cut into small cubes, usually about 1.5 cm.

Dice: to cut into cubes or dice of even size, about 5 mm.

Drizzle: to pour liquid over food in a fine stream, making a zigzag pattern over the surface.

Dust: to sprinkle lightly with flour, chopped parsley or other fine ingredients.

Flake: to separate cooked fish or meat into small pieces.

Frying: consists of three main types. Dry frying requires only enough butter or oil to just cover the base of the pan. Shallow frying requires enough oil or butter to a depth of about 5 mm depending on the food to be fried. Deep-frying requires enough oil to completely cover the food being fried. The temperature should never be above 170°C. All deep-fried foods should be drained on absorbent paper.

Glaze: to give a shine to the surface of food by coating with syrup, jam, meat juices, egg, milk or gelatine.

Grilling: to subject food to radiant heat from elements or barbecue coals. The grill should always be preheated for several minutes before cooking commences.

Julienne: thin sticks of vegetables, fruits and other foods. The term is also given to this method of cutting.

Marinate: to leave meat, poultry or fish in a tenderising or flavouring solution for a period of time.

Poach: to cook very gently in a liquid that barely simmers.

Purée: to mash and/or sieve food to give a smooth consistency. This is often done in an electric blender or food processor. Alternatively, the food can be passed through a sieve.

Sauté: to lightly fry a small amount of food at a time in butter or oil while stirring to ensure even cooking.

Simmer: to cook in liquid over low heat just below boiling point.

Steam: to cook in steam on a rack or similar in a covered pan over boiling water.

Stir-fry: to cook food quickly in a small amount of oil over high heat, stirring constantly.

Zest: the finely grated rind of citrus fruit.

CULINARY TERMS

cake pan: cake tin/baking pan

caster/castor sugar: fine granulated sugar, superfine sugar

coriander: cilantro, Chinese parsley

cornflour: cornstarch

courgette: zucchini

eggplant: aubergine

essence: extract

frying pan: skillet

grill: broil

hard-boiled egg: hard-cooked egg

icing sugar: confectioners'/powdered sugar

minced meat: ground meat

pawpaw: papaya

peppers: capsicums/sweet peppers

raw prawns: green/prawns, shrimps

rockmelon: cantaloupe

seed: pit

sieve: strain

spring onions: scallions, green onions

standard flour: plain flour/all-purpose flour

tomato paste: concentrated tomato paste

tomato purée: tomato sauce (USA)

Index